T0194683

An Analysis of

Søren Kierkegaard's

The Sickness Unto Death

Shirin Shafaie

Published by Macat International Ltd
24:13 Coda Centre, 189 Munster Road, London SW6 6AW.

Distributed exclusively by Routledge
2 Park Square, Milton Park, Abingdon, Oxon OX14 4RN
711 Third Avenue, New York, NY 10017, USA

Routledge is an imprint of the Taylor & Francis Group, an informa business

www.macat.com
info@macat.com

Cataloguing in Publication Data
A catalogue record for this book is available from the British Library.
Library of Congress Cataloguing-in-Publication Data is available upon request.
Cover illustration: Capucine Deslouis

ISBN 978-1-912303-05-2 (hardback)
ISBN 978-1-912127-40-5 (paperback)
ISBN 978-1-912281-93-0 (e-book)

CONTENTS

WAYS IN TO THE TEXT

Who Was Søren Kierkegaard? 9

What Does *The Sickness Unto Death* Say? 10

Why Does *The Sickness Unto Death* Matter? 12

SECTION 1: INFLUENCES

Module 1: The Author and the Historical Context 15

Module 2: Academic Context 21

Module 3: The Problem 27

Module 4: The Author's Contribution 33

SECTION 2: IDEAS

Module 5: Main Ideas 39

Module 6: Secondary Ideas 44

Module 7: Achievement 49

Module 8: Place in the Author's Work 54

SECTION 3: IMPACT

Module 9: The First Responses 61

Module 10: The Evolving Debate 66

Module 11: Impact and Influence Today 72

Module 12: Where Next? 77

Glossary of Terms 83

People Mentioned in the Text 87

Works Cited 92

THE MACAT LIBRARY

The Macat Library is a series of unique academic explorations of seminal works in the humanities and social sciences – books and papers that have had a significant and widely recognised impact on their disciplines. It has been created to serve as much more than just a summary of what lies between the covers of a great book. It illuminates and explores the influences on, ideas of, and impact of that book. Our goal is to offer a learning resource that encourages critical thinking and fosters a better, deeper understanding of important ideas.

Each publication is divided into three Sections: Influences, Ideas, and Impact. Each Section has four Modules. These explore every important facet of the work, and the responses to it.

This Section-Module structure makes a Macat Library book easy to use, but it has another important feature. Because each Macat book is written to the same format, it is possible (and encouraged!) to cross-reference multiple Macat books along the same lines of inquiry or research. This allows the reader to open up interesting interdisciplinary pathways.

To further aid your reading, lists of glossary terms and people mentioned are included at the end of this book (these are indicated by an asterisk [*] throughout) – as well as a list of works cited.

Macat has worked with the University of Cambridge to identify the elements of critical thinking and understand the ways in which six different skills combine to enable effective thinking.
Three allow us to fully understand a problem; three more give us the tools to solve it. Together, these six skills make up the **PACIER** model of critical thinking. They are:

ANALYSIS – understanding how an argument is built
EVALUATION – exploring the strengths and weaknesses of an argument
INTERPRETATION – understanding issues of meaning

CREATIVE THINKING – coming up with new ideas and fresh connections
PROBLEM-SOLVING – producing strong solutions
REASONING – creating strong arguments

To find out more, visit **WWW.MACAT.COM.**

CRITICAL THINKING AND *THE SICKNESS UNTO DEATH*

Primary critical thinking skill: INTERPRETATION
Secondary critical thinking skill: CREATIVE THINKING

Søren Kierkegaard's *Sickness Unto Death* is widely recognized as one of the most significant and influential works of Christian philosophy written in the nineteenth century.

One of the cornerstones of Kierkegaard's reputation as a writer and thinker, it is also a masterclass in the art of interpretation. In critical thinking, interpretation is all about defining and clarifying terms – making sure everyone is on the same page. But it can also be about redefining terms: showing old concepts in a new light by interpreting them in a certain way. This skill is at the heart of *Sickness Unto Death*. Kierkegaard's book focuses on the meaning of "despair" – the sickness named in the title. For Kierkegaard, the key problem of existence was an individual's relationship with God, and he defines true despair as equating to the idea of sin – something that separates people from God, or from the idea of a higher standard beyond ourselves.

Kierkegaard's interpretative journey into the ideas of despair, sin and death is a Christian exploration of the place of the individual in the world. But its interpretative skills inspired generations of philosophers of all stripes – including notorious atheists like Jean-Paul Sartre.

ABOUT THE AUTHOR OF THE ORIGINAL WORK

Born in Copenhagen, Denmark, in 1813, **Søren Kierkegaard** rarely left his hometown, traveling only to study briefly with philosophers in Germany. He never married, ending a brief engagement because he feared the commitment would interfere with his work. Inherited wealth allowed Kierkegaard to self-publish and he did so prolifically, mostly using a variety of pseudonyms. Yet, because he wrote in Danish, the philosopher remained relatively unknown outside of Denmark until his works were translated into English and German in the early twentieth century. He died in 1855, aged just 42.

ABOUT THE AUTHOR OF THE ANALYSIS

Dr Shirin Shafaie holds masters degrees in philosophy and middle eastern studies from the Univeristy of Tehran and SOAS. She took her PhD in politics at SOAS where she now teaches in the Department of Politics and International Studies.

ABOUT MACAT

GREAT WORKS FOR CRITICAL THINKING

Macat is focused on making the ideas of the world's great thinkers accessible and comprehensible to everybody, everywhere, in ways that promote the development of enhanced critical thinking skills.

It works with leading academics from the world's top universities to produce new analyses that focus on the ideas and the impact of the most influential works ever written across a wide variety of academic disciplines. Each of the works that sit at the heart of its growing library is an enduring example of great thinking. But by setting them in context – and looking at the influences that shaped their authors, as well as the responses they provoked – Macat encourages readers to look at these classics and game-changers with fresh eyes. Readers learn to think, engage and challenge their ideas, rather than simply accepting them.

'Macat offers an amazing first-of-its-kind tool for interdisciplinary learning and research. Its focus on works that transformed their disciplines and its rigorous approach, drawing on the world's leading experts and educational institutions, opens up a world-class education to anyone.'

Andreas Schleicher
Director for Education and Skills, Organisation for Economic Co-operation and Development

'Macat is taking on some of the major challenges in university education ... They have drawn together a strong team of active academics who are producing teaching materials that are novel in the breadth of their approach.'

Prof Lord Broers,
former Vice-Chancellor of the University of Cambridge

'The Macat vision is exceptionally exciting. It focuses upon new modes of learning which analyse and explain seminal texts which have profoundly influenced world thinking and so social and economic development. It promotes the kind of critical thinking which is essential for any society and economy. This is the learning of the future.'

Rt Hon Charles Clarke, former UK Secretary of State for Education

'The Macat analyses provide immediate access to the critical conversation surrounding the books that have shaped their respective discipline, which will make them an invaluable resource to all of those, students and teachers, working in the field.'

Professor William Tronzo, University of California at San Diego

WAYS IN TO THE TEXT

KEY POINTS

- The philosopher Søren Kierkegaard was born in Copenhagen, Denmark, in 1813 and died there 42 years later. During his life, he left Copenhagen only briefly, making short trips to Berlin to study under philosophers there.

- Kierkegaard published *The Sickness Unto Death* under a pseudonym in 1849, when he was 36. But his work did not reach a wide community of philosophers until the twentieth century, when scholars translated it into German and English.

- Kierkegaard shifted the focus of philosophy. He was the first to consider the questions of existence as they relate to a single individual, rather than the more abstract "world spirit"* that philosophers before him analyzed. In The Sickness Unto Death he contemplates the problem of the despairing individual, finding the solution in Christian faith.

Who Was Søren Kierkegaard?

Born in Copenhagen, the capital of Denmark, in 1813, Søren Kierkegaard rarely left his hometown. He made only a few short visits to study under German philosophers in the city of Berlin. He did not expect to live past the age of 34, but he survived another eight years, dying in Copenhagen in 1855.

Søren's father Michael* carried a deep sense of guilt because as a child he had cursed God. Michael believed that his family's tragedies— including the premature deaths of most of his children—were God's punishment for this youthful transgression.

Søren Kierkegaard's one romantic relationship proved unhappy and left a deep impression on him. He fell in love with a young woman named Regine Olsen* and asked her to marry him, but he broke off the engagement suddenly about a year later, fearing that marriage would interfere with what he saw as his life's mission: devotion to God and the study of theology. In *The Sickness Unto Death*, he puts forward a solution to the problem of human despair. Seeing such despair as a failure to recognize an eternal element in ourselves, Kierkegaard identifies the solution: Christian faith.

During the nineteenth century, other philosophers—especially the German idealist* philosopher G. W. F. Hegel*—attained much more fame than Kierkegaard. In the early twentieth century, scholars translated the latter's books from Danish into German and English. Once Kierkegaard's ideas received broader exposure in the philosophical community, they quickly became essential elements of modern philosophical movements, especially existentialism.*

What Does *The Sickness Unto Death* Say?

As one of the first philosophers to champion the individual, Kierkegaard's work stood in stark contrast to the dominant philosophy of his time, Hegel's absolute idealism.* Hegel focused on "world spirit" (*Weltgeist*) and did not recognize the significance of the individual.

Hegel's methods inspired Kierkegaard, but he did not agree with the conclusions of the German philosopher. In fact, he made it his life's work to combat Hegel's systemic and abstract approach. Kierkegaard shifted the focus of philosophy to concrete problems experienced in individual human life.

In Kierkegaard's day, the state did not just run the civil government. It also oversaw the dominant religious institution, the Church of Denmark. Kierkegaard called the institutional church "Christendom"* and criticized it for enforcing uniformity in its worship. He felt this created complacency among the faithful, removing any incentives for them to form their own unique relationships with God. He argued that for an individual to become fully human, he or she had to actively and personally see him or herself as related to God and answerable only to Him. A person could not just blindly accept the Church's—or "Christendom's"—view of the truth. Nor could someone substitute a speculative system of thought for his or her own intellectual and theological journey toward the recognition of God.

Kierkegaard subtitled this work *A Christian Psychological Exposition of Edification and Awakening*. And indeed he describes a path of psychological development resulting in the resolution of human despair and personal awakening. He sees Christian faith as necessary for this process of awakening and argues that only through personal devotion to God do we become fully human.

Most theologians of Kierkegaard's time—and indeed many in our own—define "sin" as particular acts of wrongdoing. Kierkegaard, by contrast, equates sin with a state of despair in which most of us find ourselves, even if we do not feel like we are in despair. Theologians generally hold that the opposite of sin is virtue, but for Kierkegaard the opposite of sin is faith. This remains one of the most original arguments in *The Sickness Unto Death*: sin is a state in which virtually everyone finds themselves and one that can be remedied only by active faith.

Through his analysis of the human condition, Kierkegaard leads the reader to his central idea: Despair is not an illness, something to eradicate. Rather, it is a necessary stage of spiritual development. Every human being must pass through this stage on the way to establishing an authentic relationship with God. In Kierkegaard's view, religious existence is the highest form of being. The ultimate goal of any serious Christian must be to see him- or herself as standing before God. This, to Kierkegaard, represents true Christianity, not the conformist "Christendom" of the institutional church. To achieve this—to "stand alone before God"—one must be conscious of one's selfhood in a specific way. Proper selfhood for Kierkegaard is not just a relation to oneself, but a relation between oneself and God that is conscious of itself as this relation.

The problem of despair remains central to philosophical debates even today. However, the existentialists who championed Kierkegaard in the first half of the twentieth century shifted the perspective away from Kierkegaard's firmly faith-based philosophy. Existentialists viewed human despair as an inevitable part of the human condition rather than as something that can be overcome through faith.

Why Does *The Sickness Unto Death* Matter?

Kierkegaard countered the dominant philosophers of his time when he placed the individual at the center of his philosophy. He defined despair as inherent to the human condition, though something that can be overcome through a trajectory of psychological development, culminating in religious faith. Moreover, he empowered—indeed, required—individuals to take responsibility for their own spiritual development in order to overcome the situation of despair in which everyone finds themselves, often unbeknownst to themselves.

In the nineteenth century, these ideas were revolutionary—or they would have been seen as revolutionary had they reached Kierkegaard's peers in the intellectual centers of Europe. However, his works, including *The Sickness Unto Death*, did not receive wide exposure until the early twentieth century, when scholars translated them into German and English.

Kierkegaard is considered to be the father of existentialism, even though that philosophical and cultural movement did not develop until nearly a century after his death. In post-World War II* Europe, the state had obliterated the individual—in some cases, literally. Kierkegaard's works, with the responsible individual occupying a central place, provided just the kind of intellectual fodder existentialists required to construct a philosophy they considered much needed. Existentialists analyzed human existence in relation to despair, anxiety, responsibility, and death—just as Kierkegaard had. Unlike Kierkegaard, however, they did this without dependence on God.

Although Christian faith has a central role in Kierkegaard's philosophy, one does not need to believe in Christianity—or in any other religion—to find inspiration in his writings. His profound analysis of despair, anxiety, and death are relevant and instructive to any thoughtful human being. Also, without adopting Christian faith, reading Kierkegaard's *Sickness Unto Death* can be a profoundly awakening experience.

SECTION 1
INFLUENCES

MODULE 1
THE AUTHOR AND THE HISTORICAL CONTEXT

KEY POINTS

- Readers from many different times and places can connect with the themes of *The Sickness Unto Death* because of its engagement with timeless and universal issues such as the human self, anxiety, despair, and faith.

- Kierkegaard inherited from his father a sense of melancholy, angst, and guilt, and a passion for both philosophical imagination and argument.

- The author leveled some of his strongest criticisms against "Christendom"* and the German school of absolute idealism.*

Why Read This Text?

Søren Abaye Kierkegaard's *The Sickness Unto Death: A Christian Psychological Exposition for Edification and Awakening*, published in 1849, fits squarely into the author's substantial catalog of theological, philosophical, psychological, and literary writings.[1] Philosophers consider Kierkegaard the father of (Christian) existentialism* because of his particular analysis of human nature. Kierkegaard did not use the term "existentialism" himself. The term was initially coined by Gabriel Marcel* in a 1943 review of Jean-Paul Sartre's* *Being and Nothingness.*[2] In fact, the existential school of philosophy did not arise until the twentieth century, long after his death. Anyone interested in exploring this influential school of philosophical thought must surely read Kierkegaard.

Kierkegaard's contemporaries did not appreciate *The Sickness Unto*

> **❝** The nineteenth-century Danish philosopher Søren Kierkegaard was one of the most gifted, creative, and provocative thinkers within the Western philosophical tradition. His books challenge and inspire readers to think differently—not only about human existence in general, but about their own lives. **❞**
>
> Clare Carlise, *Kierkegaard: A Guide for the Perplexed*

Death. And his works—including *The Sickness Unto Death*—did not attract much notice in philosophical circles outside Scandinavia. Once his books were translated into German and English in the early twentieth century, however, Kierkegaard began to attract the attention of leading German and French existentialist thinkers such as Martin Heidegger,* Albert Camus,* and Jean-Paul Sartre. Kierkegaard's engagement with timeless issues such as the human self, anxiety, despair, and faith has also drawn many social psychologists, cultural critics, and artists to his work.[3]

Universities around the world—including those in non-Western countries—continue to teach *The Sickness Unto Death*. Despite the author's insistence on the Christian faith as the sole cure for humanity's anxiety and despair, even non-Christians find much to ponder in Kierkegaard's work.

Author's Life

Born on May 5, 1813 to a wealthy family in Copenhagen, Denmark,[4] Søren Kierkegaard was the youngest of seven siblings, five of whom died before reaching the age of 34. This family tragedy contributed to his sense of melancholia and anxiety. His father, Michael P. Kierkegaard,* greatly influenced his thinking and sense of selfhood. He was a strict and pious father who kept his son in the house. He often took his son on "philosophical walks" in their front room during which the young Kierkegaard would imagine different scenes and events. This nourished Kierkegaard's imagination, and later fed into his work as a poet, theologian, and philosopher. (Kierkegaard made almost no mention of his mother, Ane Sørensdatter Lund, in his writings. She had worked as a maid in the household before becoming pregnant and marrying his father.)

Søren's father also planted in him a strong sense of guilt and angst. As a young boy, his father had worked as a shepherd. Once he had become so frustrated with the work that he had cursed God. Both Søren and his father believed that God had punished him for this early act of defiance. They saw the premature death of Søren's siblings as proof of this punishment. Søren believed that he too was destined to die before reaching the age of 34, so he made every attempt to publish as much as possible before reaching that age. On May 5, 1847, Kierkegaard noted in his diary: "How strange that I have turned thirty-four. It is utterly inconceivable to me. I was so sure that I would die before or on this birthday that I could actually be tempted to suppose that the date of my birth has been erroneously recorded and that I will still die on my thirty-fourth."[5] He died on November 11, 1855, at the age of 42.

Another influential figure in Kierkegaard's life was a young woman named Regine Olsen.* Although Kierkegaard proposed to her in 1840, he subsequently broke off the engagement less than a year later, believing he should devote his life to God and theology instead. However, Regine remained a constant source of inspiration in his life. He never married or had children and left most of his belongings to her in his will.

Between 1830 and 1840, Kierkegaard studied theology at Copenhagen University. In 1834, he experienced a sudden existential crisis and began to have serious doubts about the Christian faith. He even doubted whether he should finish his theological studies. However, after his father died in 1838, Kierkegaard decided to finish his degree and wrote his doctoral dissertation, *On the Concept of Irony with Constant Reference to Socrates*. He had to petition the king for permission to write it in Danish. However, he was still asked to conduct the public defense of his work in Latin, which, along with German, was the pan-European language of science and scholarship in the early nineteenth century.[6] He continued to employ a sense of irony in his writing—something that is unfortunately often lost in translation. He also liked to communicate his ideas indirectly.[7] In fact, he often published under pseudonyms*—including Victor Eremita, Constantine Constantius, Johannes de Silentio, and Johannes Climacus—sometimes even having these pseudonymous authors debate with each other in the pages of their books.

Author's Background

Kierkegaard was born into a society that had undergone significant sociopolitical and economic transformations. These included a catastrophic war with the British Empire, the bombing of Copenhagen in 1807, and national bankruptcy in 1813 (the year of Kierkegaard's birth). As Kierkegaard grew up, he saw a conformist and complacent bourgeoisie* rise from the ruins of the past feudal order.* The result was a new capitalist society under the strong influence of what he came to call "Christendom" (that is, the institutionalized Church). The pressure to conform made it difficult to become an independent individual or achieve authentic selfhood. The state also made every effort to standardize people's religious activities, particularly in congregations. In Kierkegaard's view, this rendered religious activities meaningless and ineffective.

Kierkegaard therefore leveled a significant portion of his criticism against this "Christendom" (*Christenheden*). He sharply differentiates Christendom from Christianity (*Christendommen*). For Kierkegaard, Christendom is Christianity expressed as a historical sociopolitical institution. Especially in the writings of his last years, Kierkegaard is extremely hostile to the historical spread of Christianity as "Christendom" in which thousands have been, and still are, enrolled into the Church as an institution without proper reference to living Christianly according to the New Testament.[8] He accused the State Church of promoting religious and spiritual complacency, saying it enforced this by having the Church hierarchy dictate people's spiritual activities. Kierkegaard also criticized the complacency and conformism of the Danish bourgeoisie, whom he saw as mutely submitting to the official Christianity, comfortably "reassured of their salvation by the clergy."[9]

From a philosophical perspective, Danish society of the early nineteenth century was dominated by Hegel's* absolute idealism.* As a systemic and speculative philosophy, absolute idealism did not recognize the significance of the individual. Throughout his intellectual career, Kierkegaard reacted against Hegelianism* and Hegel's prominent Danish adherents.

In this religious and intellectual environment, dominated by Hegelianism and "Christendom," Kierkegaard published *The Sickness Unto Death*, under the pseudonym of Anti-Climacus, in 1849. He aimed to champion the primacy of "the single specific individual" as opposed to "the crowd" in matters of religion and philosophy.

NOTES

1   Søren Kierkegaard [Anti-Climacus, pseud.], *The Sickness Unto Death: A Christian Psychological Exposition for Edification and Awakening*, trans. Alastair Hannay (London: Penguin Classics, 1989).

2   See: Felicity Joseph, Jack Reynolds, and Ashley Woodward, *The Bloomsbury Companion to Existentialism* (London: Bloomsbury Publishing, 2014), 3.

3   See for example: Jon Bartley Stewart, ed., *Kierkegaard and Existentialism* (Farnham: Ashgate Publishing, 2011); Michael Weston, *Kierkegaard and Modern Continental Philosophy: An Introduction* (London: Routledge, 1994); and Steven Crowell, ed., *The Cambridge Companion to Existentialism* (New York: Cambridge University Press, 2012).

4   For Kierkegaard's biographical information, see: Peter Rohde, *Søren Kierkegaard: An Introduction to His Life and Philosophy*, trans. Alan Moray Williams (London: Allen & Unwin, 1963); Alastair Hannay, *Kierkegaard: A Biography* (Cambridge: Cambridge University Press, 2003); and Joakim Garff, *Søren Kierkegaard: A Biography*, trans. Bruce H. Kirmmse (Princeton: Princeton University Press, 2007).

5   Garff, *Søren Kierkegaard*, 137.

6   Kierkegaard's thesis is available in English. See: Søren Kierkegaard, *Kierkegaard's Writings, II: The Concept of Irony, with Continual Reference to Socrates/Notes of Schelling's Berlin Lectures*, eds. Howard V. Hong and Edna H. Hong (Princeton: Princeton University Press, 1992).

7   See: Roger Poole, *Kierkegaard: The Indirect Communication* (Charlottesville: University of Virginia Press, 1993).

8   Julia Watkin, *The A to Z of Kierkegaard's Philosophy* (Lanham, MD: Scarecrow Press, 2000), 45–6. See also Kierkegaard's own work on the subject: Søren Kierkegaard and H. A. Johnson, *Attack Upon Christendom*, trans. Walter Macon Lowrie (Princeton: Princeton University Press, 1968).

9   Kierkegaard, *Sickness Unto Death*, 88.

MODULE 2
ACADEMIC CONTEXT

KEY POINTS

- Hegel's* philosophy deals with the abstract and absolute category of world spirit.* In absolute idealism,* Hegel makes no distinction between the rational and the real, subject and object, thought and existence.
- German absolute idealism dominated Western philosophy in the early nineteenth century.
- Hegel's dialectical* method inspired Kierkegaard, but he rejected Hegel's absolute and abstract approach to philosophy and theology.

The Work in its Context

Søren Kierkegaard's *The Sickness Unto Death: A Christian Psychological Exposition for Edification and Awakening* was not the first work to discuss the dialectics of the self, a logical analysis of what it means to be a self. Hegel had proposed a dialectics of the spirit in his first major work, *Phenomenology of Spirit* (1807).[1] Hegel though wrote in the context of the absolute and abstract category of world spirit (*Weltgeist*), not in relation to the idea of an individual human spirit. In Hegel's system, the whole of existence was set out in paragraphs and explained; he described historical development, including Christianity, as "stages in an evolutionary process bearing the stamp of necessity and expressing the realization of the world spirit, which in its turn is an expression of pure thought."[2]

Although Kierkegaard did not agree with Hegel's systemic and purely speculative approach, Hegel's dialectical method of analysis did inspire him.[3] Kierkegaard championed the primacy of the single

> ❝ Most of the more important philosophic movements since [Hegel's] death have been so many reactions against Hegel's own idealism and cannot be fully understood without some grasp of his philosophy. The first two great revolts were those of Kierkegaard and Marx, who swallowed easily as much of his philosophy as they rejected: notably, his dialectic. ❞
>
> Walter Arnold Kaufmann, *From Shakespeare to Existentialism: An Original Study*

specific individual both in his philosophy and in matters of religion. For him, to become fully human is not possible merely by thinking. On the contrary, to be truly human, Kierkegaard believed that a person had to take action and become personally responsible directly to God.

Kierkegaard was the first philosopher whose writings seriously challenged Hegelianism. Hegel had an enormous influence on nineteenth-century Western philosophy, while Kierkegaard remained relatively unknown outside his native Denmark. Despite this imbalance in reputations, Kierkegaard, and not the more famous German, would set the tone for the emerging philosophies of the twentieth century, especially existentialism.*

Overview of the Field

Many philosophies of the eighteenth century—for example, the works of the German philosopher Immanuel Kant* and the Scottish thinker David Hume*—had integrated an acceptance of the limits of human knowledge and boundaries of natural sciences into their systems of thought. But German idealism* however broke away from these limitations focusing on a metaphysical* (as opposed to a natural) concept of spirit. They also embraced the possibility that individuals might attain absolute (self-) consciousness. In fact, they considered this consciousness of self a logical necessity.

Under the influence of Hegel, intellectuals of the early nineteenth century came to see "the rational" and "the real" as one and the same. Followers of German idealism saw no real difference between reality and the spirit. This blurred the distinction between logic and metaphysics, subject and object, thought and being. As a result, early nineteenth-century philosophers became increasingly detached from real human concerns such as despair, anxiety, and angst.

In the introduction to his *Lectures on the Philosophy of World History*, Hegel makes a number of claims that illustrate how German idealists viewed the status and insignificance of the single individual. According to Hegel, "Reason cannot stop to consider the injuries sustained by single individuals, for the particular ends are submerged in the universal end."[4] And, "The individual may well be treated unjustly; but this is a matter of indifference to world history, which uses individuals only as instruments to further its own progress."[5]

The world of philosophy had become a hostile environment for the concept of the "individual human being." This is the context from which Kierkegaard's individualist philosophy of the self emerged.

Academic Influences

Kierkegaard studied theology and philosophy at Copenhagen University. During his time there, the faculty was dominated by Hegelian professors such as H. L. Martensen* and J. L. Heiberg.* A staunch Hegelian theologian, Martensen believed that it is "possible to unite faith and thought and create an all-comprehending synthesis in which all oppositions could be reconciled."[6]

Kierkegaard made it his life's work to combat Hegel's systemic and abstract approach to philosophy, theology, and faith although he was also deeply inspired by Hegel. He even confessed to an ambivalent sense of admiration for him, writing in his journal: "I feel what for me at times is an enigmatic respect for Hegel; I have learned much from him, and I know very well that I can still learn much more from him when I return to him again … His philosophical knowledge, his amazing learning, the insight of his genius, and everything else good that can be said of a philosopher I am willing to acknowledge as any disciple.—Yet, no, not *acknowledge*—this is too distinguished an expression—willing to admire, willing to learn from him."[7]

After defending his doctoral thesis, Kierkegaard—who rarely left Copenhagen—made four visits to Berlin to attend lectures by various influential philosophers including Friedrich Wilhelm Joseph Schelling.*[8] Schelling was one of the thinkers "who most likely stimulated Kierkegaard's association of the concept of anxiety with original sin and human freedom, although his own deep-seated melancholy undoubtedly also attuned him to discern the spiritual significance of this phenomenon in human existence."[9]

The ancient Greek philosopher Socrates* provided another, more positive, source of influence and philosophical inspiration for Kierkegaard. In fact, Kierkegaard relied heavily on Socrates in his doctoral dissertation: *The Concept of Irony, with Continual Reference to Socrates*.[10] In the dissertation, Kierkegaard used Socrates's conception of irony to critique Hegel's uncompromising emphasis on the supremacy of the universal. For Kierkegaard, as also "for Socrates, irony is not a movement or phase of world history and its overcoming is not achieved by the Spirit or through the concrete universal. But rather irony is an individual manifestation and is overcome through the concrete individual."[11] Kierkegaard also employed and revived Socrates's idea of irony through his use of dialogue and indirect communication.

Moreover, for Kierkegaard, irony was not a mere verbal strategy. In fact, it was a way of life.[12] Kierkegaard saw Socrates as a courageous figure who stood firmly against the established order. Socratic subjectivity was exactly the sort of "ethico-religious subjectivity" that

Kierkegaard set out to explore in his works, especially in his text titled *Postscript*.[13] For Kierkegaard, irony served as "an alternative to both the theoretical complacency of Hegelianism and the practical complacency of Christendom."[14]

NOTES

1   Georg Wilhelm Friedrich Hegel, *Phenomenology of Spirit*, trans. A. V. Miller (Oxford: Clarendon Press, 1977).

2   Peter Rohde, *Søren Kierkegaard: An Introduction to His Life and Philosophy*, trans. Alan Moray Williams (London: Allen & Unwin, 1963), 105–6.

3   For more information on Hegel's philosophy, see: Walter Kaufmann, *Hegel: A Reinterpretation* (Notre Dame, Ind.: University of Notre Dame Press, 1988); and Allen Speight, *The Philosophy of Hegel* (Montreal: McGill Queens University Press, 2008). On the relationship between Kierkegaard's thought and Hegel's philosophy, see: Mark C. Taylor, *Journeys to Selfhood: Hegel and Kierkegaard* (New York: Fordham University Press, 2000); Merold Westphal, "Kierkegaard and Hegel," in *The Cambridge Companion to Kierkegaard*, eds. Alastair Hannay and Gordon Daniel Marino (Cambridge: Cambridge University Press, 1997), 101–24; and Clare Carlisle, *Kierkegaard: A Guide for the Perplexed* (London: Bloomsbury, 2006).

4   Georg Wilhelm Friedrich Hegel, *Lectures on the Philosophy of World History* (Cambridge: Cambridge University Press, 1975), 43.

5   Hegel, *Philosophy of World History*, 65.

6   Peter Rohde, *Søren Kierkegaard: An Introduction to His Life and Philosophy*, trans. Alan Moray Williams (London: Allen & Unwin, 1963), 31.

7   Søren Kierkegaard, *Kierkegaard's Writings, XII: Concluding Unscientific Postscript to Philosophical Fragments*, eds. Howard V. Hong and Edna H. Hong (Princeton: Princeton University Press, 2013), 74.

8   Alastair Hannay, in Søren Kierkegaard [Anti-Climacus, pseud.], *The Sickness Unto Death: A Christian Psychological Exposition for Edification and Awakening*, trans. Alastair Hannay (London: Penguin Classics, 1989), 28.

9   Sylvia Walsh, *Kierkegaard: Thinking Christianly in an Existential Mode* (Oxford: Oxford University Press, 2009), 90.

10 Søren Kierkegaard, *Kierkegaard's Writings, II: The Concept of Irony, with Continual Reference to Socrates/Notes of Schelling's Berlin Lectures,* eds. Howard V. Hong and Edna H. Hong (Princeton: Princeton University Press, 1992).

11 Robert L. Perkins, "Hegel and Kierkegaard: Two Critics of Romantic Irony," *Review of National Literatures* 1, no. 2 (Fall 1970): 250–1.

12 Andrew Cross, "Neither Either Nor Or: The Perils of Reflexive Irony," in *The Cambridge Companion*, Hannay and Marino, 125–53.

13 Søren Kierkegaard, *Concluding Unscientific Postscript to Philosophical Fragments, Volume 1*, trans. Howard V. Hong and Edna H. Hong (Princeton: Princeton University Press, 1992).

14 Merold Westphal, "Kierkegaard and Hegel," in *The Cambridge Companion*, Hannay and Marino, 105.

THE PROBLEM

KEY POINTS

- The major thinkers of early nineteenth-century Denmark were debating whether speculative and systemic philosophy or Christian theology best expressed the truth.

- Kierkegaard was deeply influenced by the debate between Bishop Mynster* and Hegelian academics of his time, especially regarding Mynster's use of the Aristotelian* principle of non-contradiction.* Kierkegaard used this principle in the title of his later work *Either/Or.*

- Hegel* focused on absolute and abstract categories. Kierkegaard shifted the debate to the "single specific individual" and issues of real human existence, chief among them the problem of despair.

Core Question

Søren Kierkegaard wrote *The Sickness Unto Death: A Christian Psychological Exposition for Edification and Awakening* and his other works at a time when most philosophers and theologians were influenced by G. W. F. Hegel's philosophy of absolute idealism.*[1] The principal question of the time was how to reach truth—truth being understood as an absolute and idealist category. Kierkegaard reformulated this question in two important and original ways. First, he changed the subject of the debate, shifting the focus from the realm of abstract and absolute categories of the Hegelian philosophy such as Being, Nothing, and Becoming, to that of the "single specific individual." Second, he rejected the speculative and systemic approach of absolute idealism. He also rejected the purely theological and Church-centric

> ❝ In the 1830s, when Kierkegaard was studying at the University of Copenhagen, Hegel's philosophy was fresh, exciting and controversial. Some philosophers and theologians embraced the new system of thought, while others who rejected it tended to defend traditional Aristotelian logic against the Hegelian emphasis on the historicality of truth, and against the idea of mediation. ❞
>
> Clare Carlisle, *Kierkegaard: A Guide for the Perplexed*

approach taken by figures such as Bishop J. P. Mynster. He saw both as inadequate in terms of answering the most important questions of human existence.

Kierkegaard asked instead how we are to understand the human experience of despair, anxiety, and angst. He framed the question in terms of an individual, standing alone before God. Kierkegaard argued that to become an authentic self and to arrive at truth about oneself, one has to take action. Especially as a Christian, one cannot just erect a speculative system of pure thought or allow the Church to act as a proxy between oneself and God; one has to actively adopt faith, see oneself as directly related to God, and express this in one's actions.

In *The Sickness Unto Death*, Kierkegaard focuses on this set of questions by examining the problem of *human* despair. He discusses two types of despair, which have different degrees of intensity. The first, most common, form of despair occurs when "the defences against conscious selfhood are most effectively deployed, and where the level of self-awareness is correspondingly low."[2] When people face a difficult situation in daily life—such as the end of a romance or financial trouble—they can experience despair. The second form of despair represents one of the most original aspects of Kierkegaard's thought. This type of despair goes beyond mundane experiences and has to do with the human condition itself.

Kierkegaard thinks everyone is in a state of profound despair—whether we are aware of it or not—if we fail to recognize the eternal element in ourselves. The eternal element is the relation we have toward God; only when we recognize this relation and submit to it, can this more fundamental despair be brought to an end. The denial of "everything Christian: sin, the forgiveness of sin, etc." Kierkegaard thinks, "is the 'height' of despair."[3] In short, therefore, Kierkegaard shifted the focus from abstract categories of Hegel's philosophy to concrete problems of human life, especially to a deep form of human despair.

The Participants

Even though Hegelianism* dominated the Danish intellectual environment of the early nineteenth century, some people rejected this approach, most notably Bishop Mynster. Mynster had a very good command of the Hegelian philosophical and logical issues and made it clear that his religious beliefs "provide[d] the foundation for his thinking. His attitude to philosophy [was] quite different from the Hegelian view that philosophy provides the highest and most complete expression of the truth … he [did] not think that Christianity needs philosophical support or justification for the truths expressed in the Bible. In other words, he rejected the project of Enlightenment* rationalism."[4] Therefore, "as an unsystematic and intuitive individualist … Mynster conceived an instant distaste for Hegel's systematic philosophy."[5]

The debate between Bishop Mynster and the major Hegelian thinkers J. L. Heiberg* and H. L. Martensen* kicked off in 1839 when one of Martensen's students published an article suggesting that "in theology both rationalism and supernaturalism are antiquated standpoints."[6] The writer proposed that "the distinction between rationalism and supernaturalism—which are two alternative approaches to religious belief—can be overcome through Hegelian mediation."[7] Mynster responded by drawing "a clear distinction between these two positions and argued that contemporary Christian believers have to choose to commit to one or another [the Aristotelian principle of contradiction]." Heiberg continued the debate, writing an article that defended the Hegelian principle of mediation.[8]

Despite his contribution to the early debate on Hegelianism and his significant influence on Kierkegaard's later writings, Bishop Mynster's opposition to Hegelianism remained a mere "distaste."[9] His thinking did not develop along any revolutionary or original lines in its own right. Mynster even pointed out in his memoirs that he had "neither the inclination nor the ability" to combat Hegelianism.[10] In contrast to this studied inaction, Kierkegaard not only dared to confront Hegel's absolute idealism, he also criticized the mainstream approach to Christianity that dominated the academic, religious, and political circles of his time.

The Contemporary Debate

The debate between Bishop Mynster, on the one side, and Heiberg and Martensen on the other significantly impacted Kierkegaard's later writings. Kierkegaard opposed Hegel's absolute idealism by placing the specific single individual at the core of his own conception of the self. At the same time, he reacted to the State Church of Denmark, the institutionalized Christianity of his time, which he labeled "Christendom."* According to Kierkegaard, "Christendom" was "not only a miserable edition of Christianity, full of misprints that distort the meaning and of thoughtless omissions and emendations, but an abuse of it in having taken Christianity's name in vain."[11]

Conversely he proclaimed, "Christian heroism, and indeed one perhaps sees little enough of that, is to risk unreservedly being oneself, an individual human being, this specific individual human being alone before God, alone in this enormous exertion and this enormous accountability."[12]

Kierkegaard aimed to reintroduce a culture of critical debate into contemporary society. His principal criticism against the state of religion and philosophy was that these institutions had become complacent and conformist. He argued that Hegel's absolute idealism and the institution of "Christendom" had emptied society of critical and independent thinking. However, in deference to two of the most respected figures in his life—his father and their family priest, Bishop Mynster—he posed his critique of "Christendom" under pseudonyms. Kierkegaard criticized "Christendom" tacitly until both men had died. After their deaths, he launched a more direct and forceful attack against the State Church. Indeed, his final years were taken up with a sustained, outright attack on the Church of Denmark by means of newspaper articles published in *The Fatherland* (*Fædrelandet*) and a series of self-published pamphlets called *The Moment* (Øjeblikket), also translated as *The Instant*. *The Moment* was translated into German as well as other European languages in 1861 and again in 1896.[13]

Kierkegaard shifted the focus of attention from an absolute and idealist perspective to an essentially human perspective. This had a major impact on the contemporary debate about the central issue of despair. After Kierkegaard, the problem of despair and the idea of the absurd became central themes in philosophical debates, especially among existentialist* thinkers of the twentieth century such as Jean-Paul Sartre,* Albert Camus,* and others. Later existentialist philosophers viewed this sense of human despair and absurdity as an inherent, inevitable, and irresolvable human condition. Unlike Kierkegaard, the twentieth-century existentialists did not see despair as something that can be overcome through faith.

NOTES

1   Clare Carlisle, *Kierkegaard: A Guide for the Perplexed* (London: Bloomsbury, 2006), 52.

2   Alastair Hannay, in Søren Kierkegaard [Anti-Climacus, pseud.], Introduction to *The Sickness Unto Death: A Christian Psychological Exposition for Edification and Awakening*, trans. Alastair Hannay (London: Penguin Classics, 1989), 4.

3   Hannay, Introduction to *The Sickness Unto Death*, 4.

4   Carlisle, *Kierkegaard: A Guide*, 55.

5   Bruce H. Kirmmse, *Kierkegaard in Golden Age Denmark* (Bloomington, Ind.: Indiana University Press, 1990), 124. For Hegel's philosophy of religion, see: Georg Wilhelm Friedrich Hegel, *Hegel: Lectures on the Philosophy of Religion: Vol. I: Introduction and the Concept of Religion*, ed. Peter C. Hodgson (Oxford: Oxford University Press, 2007).

6   Carlisle, *Kierkegaard: A Guide*, 52.

7   Carlisle, *Kierkegaard: A Guide*, 52.

8   Carlisle, *Kierkegaard: A Guide*, 53.

9   Kirmmse, *Kierkegaard in Golden Age Denmark*, 124.

10 Quoted in Kirmmse, *Kierkegaard in Golden Age Denmark*, 125.

11 Kierkegaard, *Sickness Unto Death*, 134.

12 Kierkegaard, preface to *Sickness Unto Death*, 35.

13 See: Søren Kierkegaard, *The Moment and Late Writings: Kierkegaard's Writings, Vol. 23*, trans. Howard V. Hong and Edna H. Hong (Princeton: Princeton University Press, 1998). These pamphlets are now also included in Søren Kierkegaard and H. A. Johnson, *Attack Upon Christendom*, trans. Walter Macon Lowrie (Princeton: Princeton University Press, 1968).

THE AUTHOR'S CONTRIBUTION

KEY POINTS

- Kierkegaard shifted the focus of analysis in philosophy and theology from absolute and idealist categories to the "single specific individual."

- He rejected the purely speculative and systemic approaches to philosophy and theology common in the early nineteenth century.

- Kierkegaard's approach to the problem of despair was nevertheless a dialectical approach aimed at enlightening and awakening people so they could develop a higher sense of human selfhood.

Author's Aims

The full title of Søren Kierkegaard's *The Sickness Unto Death: A Christian Psychological Exposition of Edification and Awakening* clearly indicates the text's purpose. In the preface, Kierkegaard declares his intention: "In a Christian context everything, yes everything, should serve to edify. The kind of scholarship that is not in the last resort edifying is for that very reason un-Christian. An account of anything Christian must be like a physician's lecture beside the sick-bed."[1] The particular sickness that Kierkegaard explores in this book is despair. How important is it to reflect on despair? He looks at it as a universal question that reveals the true self: "If you have lived in despair, then whatever else you won or lost, for you everything is lost, eternity does not acknowledge you, it never knew you, or, still more dreadful, it knows you as you are known, it manacles you to your self in despair!"[2]

> ❝ [After Kierkegaard] No longer must theology cut itself to the size and shape allowed by an Aristotle, a Hegel, or a Kant; it need not try to incorporate positivism or a social gospel founded upon a notion of social progress. In this sense, Kierkegaard, having penetrated the smoke and haze of the accommodating and intimidated theologies of the eighteenth and early nineteenth centuries, emerges as the first post-modern theologian. ❞
>
> Robert Perkins, *Søren Kierkegaard*

In *The Sickness Unto Death*, Kierkegaard poses three interrelated questions:

- What is the human self or spirit?
- What is despair or "sickness unto death"?
- How can it be remedied?

In asking these questions Kierkegaard delves into the universal realm of human existence, its conditions and concerns. He was not the first philosopher to attend to the dialectics* of the self and spirit. But by maintaining an uncompromising focus on the "single specific individual," his approach went far beyond the dominant philosophies of his time. He wanted to bring people's attention both to their true self and to their relationship with the eternal aspect of their existence. Therefore, *The Sickness Unto Death* was not merely a critical reaction to Hegelianism* and "Christendom."* It also articulated Kierkegaard's independent and original thought on the nature of human self, the problem of despair, and the individual's relationship with God.

Approach

Two important factors mark Kierkegaard's approach as novel. First, he emphasizes the primacy of the individual human being. In

Kierkegaard's view, the individual is a synthesis between the finite and the infinite, the temporal and the eternal, necessity and freedom. In contrast to Hegel's* absolute idealism,* Kierkegaard sees the individual as developing into an authentic self only when considering oneself as standing directly before God. Kierkegaard complains that "this notion of the single human being before God never occurs to speculative thought [that] only universalizes particular humans phantastically into the human race."[3] Such an absolute and idealist view of the human being robs individuals of their freedom. In Kierkegaard's words, "where the actual individual person is not brought in, the transition occurs necessarily (based in the System that everything comes about by necessity)."[4]

Second, in analyzing the problem of despair, Kierkegaard makes an original use of the dialectical method. He proposes that despair is not an illness that we should get rid of or try to prevent. On the contrary, despair constitutes an important stage in spiritual development. In fact, it is the only avenue through which one can reach "truth and deliverance." The twentieth-century philosopher Alastair Hannay* emphasizes the importance of this aspect of Kierkegaard's approach, for "it seems to imply that human ... spiritual development is bound to progress through a state of sickness."[5] Spiritual fulfillment thus depends on the possibility of despair, and "the only way of escaping despair, therefore, seems to be to go through with it."[6] At the moment of despair, one faces two possibilities: remain in the state of despair or have faith in God and thus be cured of the sickness. "[A]lthough *The Sickness Unto Death* progressively tracks the movement away from faith in the consciousness of despair or sin, which is the opposite of faith, it also suggests that these negative factors can function dialectically in an indirectly positive manner so as to become *the first element in faith* inasmuch as one acquires the possibility of being cured from despair and sin by becoming conscious of oneself as existing before God and Christ."[7]

Contribution in Context

The Sickness Unto Death did not mark the first time Kierkegaard considered the question of despair and human selfhood. He had confronted the issue in both his first major work *Either/Or* (1843) and *The Concept of Anxiety* (1844).[8] However, in *The Concept of Anxiety* he limited the discussion to the psychological conceptualization of the self. In *The Sickness Unto Death* he conducted his inquiry of the human self on a higher, religious level.

In *The Sickness Unto Death*, Kierkegaard equates the idea of despair with that of sin. He explains why we sin in not wanting to be a self that is before God (weakness). However, an even worse sin is to deny such relationship between one's self and God and the gravest sin of all is wanting to be oneself (defiance) in the face of despair. In the course of this, Kierkegaard evolved his main unit of analysis, "the single specific individual," into a religious category conditioned by his "psychological isolation, but at the same time transcending it as a universal determination of the religious consciousness."[9] Thus the subject of despair in *The Sickness Unto Death* applies not to just any human self but to "the theological self" in particular. According to Kierkegaard, "the point is this. The progression in consciousness we have been concerned with up to now occurs within the category of the human self, or of the self that has man as its standard of measurement. But this self takes on a new quality and specification in being the self that is directly before God ... the theological self ... being conscious of being before God, by being a human self that has God as its standard!"[10]

NOTES

1   Søren Kierkegaard [Anti-Climacus, pseud.], preface to *The Sickness Unto Death: A Christian Psychological Exposition for Edification and Awakening*, trans. Alastair Hannay (London: Penguin Books, 1989), 35.

2   Kierkegaard, *Sickness Unto Death*, 57–8.

3   Kierkegaard, *Sickness Unto Death*, 115.

4   Kierkegaard, *Sickness Unto Death*, 125.

5   Alastair Hannay, in Kierkegaard, introduction to *Sickness Unto Death*, 5.

6   Alastair Hannay, in Kierkegaard, introduction to *Sickness Unto Death*, 5.

7   Sylvia Walsh, *Kierkegaard: Thinking Christianly in an Existential Mode*
     (Oxford: Oxford University Press, 2009), 159.

8   The full title of the book is *The Concept of Anxiety: A Simple Psychologically
     Oriented Reflection on the Dogmatic Problem of Original Sin by Vigilius
     Haufniensis* [another of Kierkegaard's pseudonyms].

9   In his *Point of View for My Work as an Author* he regards this category
     as the most important achievement of his work. See Louis K. Dupré,
     Kierkegaard as Theologian: The Dialectic of Christian Existence (New York:
     Sheed & Ward, 1963), 36.

10   Kierkegaard, *Sickness Unto Death*, 111.

SECTION 2
IDEAS

MAIN IDEAS

KEY POINTS

- *The Sickness Unto Death* is a book about despair, a particular kind of spiritual sickness that exists in the human self.

- In order to understand Kierkegaard's definition of despair and his solution for it, the reader must first understand his conception of the human self, which is understood as a synthesis of the infinite and the finite, of the temporal and the eternal, of freedom and necessity.

- Despair is a misrelation, or an imbalance, that occurs when the balance between these opposing factors is upset. It can be resolved, most generally, through personally choosing (Christian) faith. Thus for Kierkegaard, the opposite of being in despair is to have faith.

Key Themes

The Sickness Unto Death:A Christian Psychological Exposition of Edification and Awakening provides a comprehensive discussion of the self, the different ways of losing oneself in despair and sin, and the issue of faith. The title of the book is a quotation derived from Jesus' remark about Lazarus, a man whom Jesus raised from the dead (John 11:4). Søren Kierkegaard poses the following central question with regard to Lazarus's story: "Ah!, but even had Christ not awoken Lazarus, is it not still true that this sickness, death itself, is not unto death?"[1] For Kierkegaard the significance of Jesus' miracle was not in bringing a dead man back to life (because a man's nature makes him mortal or physically perishable), but in proving that God exists. Kierkegaard proposes that death is not the absolute end of human existence, that

> **❝** The biggest danger, that of losing oneself, can pass off in the world as quietly as if it were nothing; every other loss, an arm, a leg, five dollars, a wife, etc. is bound to be noticed. **❞**
>
> Kierkegaard, *The Sickness Unto Death*

there is hope even after death, and, therefore, that sickness is not unto death: "If, in the strictest sense, there is to be any question of a sickness unto death, it must be one where the end is death and where death is the end. And thinking that is precisely to despair."[2]

In order to explain despair as a sickness of the self (or spirit), Kierkegaard first unpacks the conception of the human self as a synthesis of dialectically* opposing factors, "of the infinite and the finite, of the temporal and the eternal, of freedom [possibility] and necessity."[3] According to him, "if there were nothing eternal in a man, he would simply be unable to despair."[4] He then discusses the idea of despair and its various forms "by reflecting on the factors which constitute the self as a synthesis."[5] Sickness unto death or despair occurs when the balance between the opposing factors is upset. Despair is the "misrelation," the lack of balance, that arises in the self when the finite and infinite, or temporal and eternal aspects of the synthesis, do not come into proper relation to one other. One may be conscious or unconscious of this despair or even of having a self. The more conscious one becomes of his or herself, the more intense will be the degree to which that person is capable of despairing.

Exploring the Ideas

The book has two parts. In Part One, "the progression in consciousness ... occurs within the category of the human self, or of the self that has man as its standard of measurement."[6] In Part Two, this self takes on a new specification by becoming "the theological self," meaning a self that is directly and consciously before God and has God as its standard. Accordingly, Kierkegaard refers to sin as a despair that applies to a self that is before God or to a self that has a conception of God.

For Kierkegaard, religious existence is the highest form of being for humankind. The religious stage comes after the natural/aesthetic and the ethical stages in the progression of the human self. Note, though, that Kierkegaard's idea of these three stages of human existence does not correspond to any automatic natural or biological development. In fact, it is possible that a person may never reach a level of existence beyond the aesthetic stage.[7] The possibility of despair is the path through which one can progress from ignorance or defiance to faith. According to Kierkegaard, "the possibility of this sickness [i.e. despair] is man's advantage over the beast; to be aware of this sickness is the Christian's advantage over natural man; to be cured of this sickness is the Christian's blessedness."[8] Here despair can lead to a "transformation in which consciousness of the eternal in the self breaks through, so that the struggle can begin which either intensifies despair to an even higher form [that is, defiance] or else leads to faith."[9]

The Sickness Unto Death provides a therapeutic resolution to despair, namely (Christian) faith. For Kierkegaard, "the opposite to being in despair is to have faith."[10] To have faith is to believe that for God everything is possible. "The decisive moment only comes when man is brought to the utmost extremity, where in human terms there is no possibility. Then the question is whether he will believe that for God everything is possible, that is, whether he will have faith."[11] If the answer is negative, then the person is bound to remain in despair. It is vital to note that Kierkegaard posits his conception of sin in opposition to faith and not virtue. According to him, "this is one of the most crucial definitions for the whole of Christianity: that the opposite of sin is not virtue but faith."[12]

Language and Expression

Kierkegaard wrote in a highly personal and enigmatic style, which aimed to bring the reader's latent ideas into a clear light. As such, one of the key exercises in approaching Kierkegaard's work is trying to comprehend exactly what it is that he is saying. This interpretative task is crucial to understanding *The Sickness Unto Death*, for it is riddled with divergent communication, inference, imaginative metaphors, and cryptic notions. This makes it very difficult to categorize Kierkegaard's thinking and reach a sustained conclusion for the whole work.

As far as the audience of the text is concerned, Kierkegaard addresses humanity as a whole. His existentialist* discourse is not bound by any specific culture, time, or place. Despite the author's overwhelming emphasis on Christianity, *The Sickness Unto Death* is not aimed at Christians exclusively. In fact, Kierkegaard's imagined audience corresponded to any individual human being, "*my reader: that single individual.*" Even though in principal Kierkegaard addresses his works toward this individual reader, the complexity of his writing makes it hard to grasp that he truly envisioned the general public as his primary audience. Kierkegaard did not adapt his writing to suit all. For this he offers the following justification in the preface to *The Sickness Unto Death*: "The form of this 'exposition' may strike many readers as odd: To them it would seem too rigorous to be edifying and too edifying to have the rigour of scholarship. On the latter I have no opinion, but regarding the former I disagree, and were it indeed too rigorous to be edifying, I would consider that a fault."[13]

Kierkegaard associates rigor with philosophical rigidity. His indirect communication— along with his adoption of pseudonyms— is a way to avoid telling readers explicitly what to believe. Instead he offers a range of positions articulated from different perspectives. In this manner, Kierkegaard aims to complicate standard philosophical or theological claims, encouraging edification rather than conformity.

NOTES

1   Søren Kierkegaard [Anti-Climacus, pseud.], *The Sickness Unto Death: A Christian Psychological Exposition for Edification and Awakening*, trans. Alastair Hannay (London: Penguin Classics, 1989), 37–8.

2   Kierkegaard, *Sickness Unto Death*, 47.

3   Kierkegaard, *Sickness Unto Death*, 43.

4   Kierkegaard, *Sickness Unto Death*, 51.

5   Kierkegaard, *Sickness Unto Death*, 59.

6   Kierkegaard, *Sickness Unto Death*, 111.

7   For a more complex explication of Kierkegaard's idea of the three stages of human existence, see: Søren Kierkegaard, *Concluding Unscientific Postscript to Philosophical Fragments, Volume 1*, trans. Howard V. Hong and Edna H. Hong (Princeton: Princeton University Press, 1992); and Søren Kierkegaard, *Kierkegaard's Writings, XI: Stages on Life's Way*, eds. Howard V. Hong and Edna H. Hong (Princeton: Princeton University Press, 2013).

8   Kierkegaard, *Sickness Unto Death*, 45.

9   Kierkegaard, *Sickness Unto Death*, 91.

10 Kierkegaard, *Sickness Unto Death*, 79.

11 Kierkegaard, *Sickness Unto Death*, 68.

12 Kierkegaard, *Sickness Unto Death*, 115.

13 Kierkegaard, *Sickness Unto Death*, 43.

SECONDARY IDEAS

KEY POINTS

- For Kierkegaard the idea of standing alone before God, and Christianity in general, implies a paradox.
- According to Kierkegaard, actually being before God is intellectually absurd.
- The category of absurd was picked up by the twentieth-century existentialist* thinkers such as Jean-Paul Sartre* and Albert Camus.*

Other Ideas

The most important secondary idea in *The Sickness Unto Death: A Christian Psychological Exposition of Edification and Awakening* is clearly marked by Søren Kierkegaard in Part Two of the book ("Despair is Sin") under an Addendum: "That the definition of sin includes the possibility of offence: a general observation about offence."[1]

In Part Two, Kierkegaard posits sin, rather than virtue, in opposition to faith. To him, "this is one of the most crucial definitions for the whole of Christianity: that the opposite of sin is not virtue but faith."[2] In the addendum to Chapter 1 of Part Two he explains why he considers this issue to be of such importance. According to him, "at the root of the opposition lies the crucial Christian specification: before God; and that in turn has the crucial Christian characteristic: the absurd, the paradox."[3] Here he makes a slight digression by introducing a new theme, namely the nature of religious offense and how the paradox of Christianity can lead either to offense or to belief.[4]

The paradox lies in the idea that God, who is eternal (that is,

> 66 The only life wasted is the life of one who so lived it, deceived by life's pleasures or its sorrows, that he never became decisively, eternally, conscious of himself as spirit, as self, or, what is the same, he never became aware—and gained in the deepest sense the impression—that there is a God there and that 'he,' himself, his self, exists before this God, which infinite gain is never come by except through despair. 99
>
> Søren Kierkegaard, *The Sickness Unto Death*

timeless), came into being in the form of Jesus Christ, lived and died (temporal events), and also that God took on the form of the least significant of men. It implies that Christianity is based on a conceptually unintelligible premise. Actually being before God is intellectually absurd.[5] Although this idea of the absurd remains secondary to Kierkegaard's main discussion of despair and sin in *The Sickness Unto Death*, it sets the stage for the twentieth-century existentialist thinkers, key among them being Jean-Paul Sartre and Albert Camus. These thinkers deeply engage with the absurdity intrinsic to the human conditions in their own work.[6]

Exploring the Ideas
Kierkegaard employed "the paradox of standing alone before God" to present his own view of "true Christianity" in opposition to institutionalized "Christendom."* In the same addendum, Kierkegaard offers the following key statement about (true) Christianity: "Christianity teaches that this single human being, whether husband, wife, servant girl, cabinet minister, merchant, barber, student, etc., this single human being, who might be proud to have spoken once in his life with the king, this human being who hasn't the least illusion of being on an intimate footing with this or that person,

this human being is before God, can talk with God any time he wants, certain of being heard; in short this human being has an invitation to live on the most intimate footing with God!"[7]

This discussion also links to the idea that denying Christianity as a religion of lies is the gravest sin. According to Kierkegaard, this sin comes about because the idea of Christianity is too grand for the natural man to be able to relate himself to it; therefore he feels offended and decides to deny it instead. The natural man (as opposed to the religious man) cannot rationally understand the incarnation of God in the figure of Jesus or his own position as standing alone before God. He finds the former a paradox and the latter absurd and thus despairs. In his despair, the natural man denies Christianity as falsehood, which is in fact the gravest sin and deepest perpetuation of despair.

The notion of a true Christian as a single human being who stands alone and directly before God compels the individual to strive toward a strong sense of responsibility, action, and genuine selfhood. A good understanding of these ideas, in addition to the conception of the religious offense and the absurd, is essential for grasping the meaning of Kierkegaard's Christian existentialism and its influence on the twentieth-century existentialist thinkers.

Overlooked

In the preface to *The Sickness Unto Death*, as in its subtitle, Kierkegaard identifies edification and awakening as his ultimate goal in writing this book.[8] This was not just a rhetorical claim but was indeed an issue at the heart of Kierkegaard's philosophy. He strongly believed in practice, especially what he identified as Christian practice,[9] as compared to pure thought. The idea of change and proactive engagement with the world is central to Kierkegaard's thought. Those aspects of Kierkegaard's thought that are specifically Christian are nevertheless to a large extent overlooked by successive thinkers such as Sartre and Camus.

Today, more than a century and a half after the first publication of *The Sickness Unto Death*, the state of the intellectual debate about the nature of human self and its universal concerns has radically changed and is ever more secularized. No longer are the theological definitions of the human self taken for granted, or regarded as necessary for authentic selfhood. There is now a lively debate among the contemporary critics of Kierkegaard in relation to his dialectics of the self and his discussion of (the Christian) faith as the sole remedy to the problem of despair. Some of the more recent critics have challenged Kierkegaard's account of authentic selfhood by asking, "Why, in any case, if selfhood is to be linked to fulfilment, should the fulfilment be specifically Christian?"[10]

In short, whereas some of the secondary ideas in Kierkegaard's thought, such as the idea of the absurd, were taken up by major philosophers and writers of the twentieth century, other central aspects of his philosophy, such as his Christian approach to the problem of despair and his faith-based formulation of the human self, are generally overlooked. A new focus on the neglected aspects of Kierkegaard's work may change not only the way in which the seminal text as a whole is understood, but also the understanding of what it means to be a single specific individual, with a distinctive eternal or divine element.

NOTES

1   Søren Kierkegaard [Anti-Climacus, pseud.], *The Sickness Unto Death: A Christian Psychological Exposition for Edification and Awakening*, trans. Alastair Hannay (London: Penguin Books, 1989), 115.

2   Kierkegaard, *Sickness Unto Death*, 115.

3   Kierkegaard, *Sickness Unto Death*, 115.

4   This theme is central to Kierkegaard's earlier works, notably *Philosophical Fragments* (1844) and *Concluding Unscientific Postscript to Philosophical Fragments* (1846), and would be discussed again in full detail in his next work, *Practice in Christianity* (1850).

5   Alastair Hannay, in Kierkegaard, introduction *Sickness Unto Death*, note

174, 59.

6   See for example: Jon Bartley Stewart, ed., *Kierkegaard and Existentialism* (Farnham: Ashgate Publishing, 2011); and Steven Crowell, ed., *The Cambridge Companion to Existentialism* (New York: Cambridge University Press, 2012).

7   Kierkegaard, *Sickness Unto Death*, 117.

8   Kierkegaard, preface to *Sickness Unto Death*, 35.

9   See also: Søren Kierkegaard, *Kierkegaard's Writings, XX: Practice in Christianity*, trans. Howard V. Hong and Edna H. Hong (Princeton: Princeton University Press, 1991).

10 Alastair Hannay, in Kierkegaard, introduction to *Sickness Unto Death*, 8.

ACHIEVEMENT

KEY POINTS

- Kierkegaard's *Sickness Unto Death* provides a comprehensive analysis of the human self, the problem of despair, and finally a therapeutic solution to it in the form of (Christian) faith.

- His untiring emphasis on the single specific individual and his or her real concerns and anxieties sets Kierkegaard apart from other philosophers and theologians before him.

- Despite his insistence on the contradiction between reason and faith, Kierkegaard was not an irrationalist. His aim was to introduce an understanding of the human self that would take into account both the temporal and eternal aspects of human existence.

Assessing the Argument

The Sickness Unto Death:A Christian Psychological Exposition of Edification and Awakening discusses the dialectics* of the self and despair through a set of empirical (that is, based on verifiable evidence) and theoretical examples. Even though Søren Kierkegaard criticizes the systemic approach to philosophy and theology, he wrote *The Sickness Unto Death* in a systemic style. However, in contrast to other popular systemic approaches such as Hegelianism,* Kierkegaard articulates his arguments in relation to the single specific individual (as opposed to the absolute spirit) and that focuses his analysis on the real concerns and fears of single human beings. He approaches these by examining real-life examples such as alcoholism, romance, and suicide. In other words, he remained true to his conviction that it is the single individual that deserves to be the subject of philosophical inquiry and not the

> 66 One lingering myth about Kierkegaard is that he is an irrationalist in some sense that denies the value of clear and honest thinking. Kierkegaard did deny the ability of reasoned thought to arrive at universal and objective truth on matters of value, but today that is considered quite rational. 99
>
> Alastair Hannay and Gordon D. Marino, introduction, *The Cambridge Companion to Kierkegaard*

absolute category of world spirit.*

Kierkegaard's dialectical conceptualization of despair is one of the most important aspects of *The Sickness Unto Death*. He differentiates between the purely emotional form of despair (which might result from mundane circumstances) and the sickness of the spirit that is an imbalance of different factors in the constitution of the human self. The latter concept of despair (this sickness of the spirit) takes on two further forms. The first is "the despair of a person for whom the situation of the solitary individual is too strenuous an ideal." The other is the despair of a person who actively rejects the ideal. They are respectively called the despairs of not wanting to be oneself and of wanting to be oneself."[1] In the first, one is unconscious of the eternal aspect in oneself. As a result, in despair one wants to be "one's *own* self, instead of a self whose specifications and identity are the outcome of one's relationship to God."[2] The second form of despair occurs "once the true nature of the ideal breaks through (once, as Kierkegaard puts it, there is 'consciousness of an infinite self'), a progressively clear-minded and deliberate refusal to accept it."[3]

Kierkegaard's reworking of the problem of despair as a sickness of the spirit allows him to make a therapeutic contribution to the problem of despair. According to Kierkegaard, one must first experience a deepened state of despair, which can come about only once one becomes fully aware of one's self, before one can experience true (Christian) faith, which he equates with the only cure for the problem of despair.[4]

Achievement in Context

The Sickness Unto Death is an example of the author's mature theological, psychological, and philosophical thought, and provides Kierkegaard's most detailed discussion of the self. Although the book did not provoke any immediate response in Danish intellectual and religious circles, it provided the groundwork for the development of a faith-based psychology. This was the work's principal achievement in its own context. As C. Stephen Evans notes, "although Kierkegaard's mission was to reintroduce Christianity to Christendom, he saw psychology as an essential element in that task. Before he could begin to communicate Christianly to people, he had to help them gain a truer perspective on what it means to exist as a human being."[5] For Kierkegaard the truly Christian way of living was closely interrelated with degrees of individual self-awareness. However, higher degrees of self-awareness do "not necessarily or automatically lead to Christian faith. A person may see his need for God and self-consciously rebel against God … but self-understanding at least makes faith a live possibility."[6]

Kierkegaard's radical revision of the idea of sin—as a state of being rather than particular acts of wrongdoing—should also be regarded as one of the text's achievements. For Kierkegaard the problem in equating sin with particular acts of wrongdoing "is not in the assertion that some acts are sins; it is the failure to see that the origin of sinful deeds lies in an underlying attitude of prideful autonomy over against God."[7] This point is underlined by Kierkegaard's insistence that faith, rather than virtue, is the opposite of sin.

Kierkegaard's psychological and subjective approach to Christianity—focusing on the human self—and his reformulation of despair as a state of being constitute the most original and significant achievements of *The Sickness Unto Death*.

Limitations

The twenty-first century has been described as an increasingly secular age.[8] The mainstream approach to politics, especially in the West, upholds the separation of religion (Church) and the state. A similar attitude exists in the social sciences and humanities, and in the physical and biological sciences. In this context, one aspect of Kierkegaard's work raises questions about the universal applicability of his unmistakably Christian outlook. Can Kierkegaard's thought be useful for non-Christians? Can it be used by followers of other religions? What can an atheist reader take from *The Sickness Unto Death*?

Kierkegaard's Christian psychology of the self—along with his faith-based therapeutic solution to the problem of despair—discusses why wanting to be a self-determining individual is worse than becoming a true self through the acceptance of God. This question becomes problematic when considered in relation to another Kierkegaardian idea: that being conscious of one's self is a form of strength if it is accompanied with a conception of God and an awareness of one's relationship with God. What is not fully clear is how overcoming despair altogether by adopting a Christian faith is *actually* possible and why it is considered to lead to a more complete and genuine form of selfhood. Did Kierkegaard not argue that to be able to despair is one of the most significant aspects of being an individual human being? If so, then how is it that overcoming despair altogether makes one more fully human? It can thus be concluded that Kierkegaard's solution to despair does not actually follow one of his central premises of what it means to be truly human, for it forgoes the ability to despair.

NOTES

1   Alastair Hannay, in Søren Kierkegaard [Anti-Climacus, pseud.], *The Sickness Unto Death: A Christian Psychological Exposition for Edification and Awakening*, trans. Alastair Hannay (London: Penguin Classics, 1989), 11.

2   Alastair Hannay, in Kierkegaard, introduction to *Sickness Unto Death*, 11.

3   Alastair Hannay, in Kierkegaard, introduction to *Sickness Unto Death*, 11.

4   Kierkegaard, *Sickness Unto Death*, 79.

5   C. Stephen Evans, *Søren Kierkegaard's Christian Psychology: Insight for Counseling and Pastoral Care* (Grand Rapids, MI: Ministry Resources Library, 1990), 22.

6   Evans, *Kierkegaard's Christian Psychology*, 21.

7   Evans, *Kierkegaard's Christian Psychology*, 57.

8   Charles Taylor, *A Secular Age* (Cambridge, MA: Harvard University Press, 2007).

PLACE IN THE AUTHOR'S WORK

KEY POINTS

- Kierkegaard's overarching philosophical question is to find out what it means to exist as a human being and how one can become a true self, that is, an authentic individual.

- Kierkegaard published many of his works, including *The Sickness Unto Death,* under pseudonyms. He thereby wished to avoid appearing as a self-proclaimed authority with a definitive religious position.

- *The Sickness Unto Death* provides Kierkegaard's most comprehensive definition of the human self and introduces the idea of the "theological self," which is a vital concept for understanding his Christian existentialism.

Positioning

Between 1838 and 1855, Søren Kierkegaard published 27 works including a whole series of edifying discourses and lectures, pamphlets, and newspaper articles, in addition to numerous diary entries, letters, and unpublished material.[1] He also published various "Discourses at the Communion on Fridays," which closely resemble sermons (although they are delivered "without authority"). These are particularly intimate addresses to the sincere Christian, who strives to deepen the subjective passion of faith through confession and through acceptance of divine forgiveness.

Kierkegaard's publications can be divided into two general categories: works written under his real name and those published under pseudonyms. His edifying discourses were often published under his own name, whereas his books were published only under

> 66 One of the most unusual and perplexing features of Kierkegaard's writing is his use of pseudonyms— not just a single pseudonym, but several different ones. These pseudonyms have distinct personalities and backgrounds: they are literary characters rather than merely pen-names. 99
>
> Clare Carlisle, *Kierkegaard: A Guide for the Perplexed*

pseudonyms (including Victor Eremita, Constantine Constantius, Johannes de Silentio, Vigilius Haufniensis, Johannes Climacus, and Anti-Climacus—the pseudonymous author of *The Sickness Unto Death: A Christian Psychological Exposition of Edification and Awakening*). He presented each pseudonym as an independent author with his own views about the given subject matter. Thereby he countered any assumption of authority by himself, especially in matters of faith. Moreover, "the pseudonymity also discourages the diversionary tendency to commit the genetic fallacy of psychologising and historicising the works as autobiography and thereby supposedly 'explaining' them."[2]

Kierkegaard leveled his strongest criticism against Hegel's* systemic philosophy when writing under the pseudonym Johannes Climacus, especially in his *Concluding Unscientific Postscript to the Philosophical Fragments: A Mimic-Pathetic-*

Dialectic Composition, an Existential Contribution (1846). The preceding *Philosophical Fragments* (1844) sought, in subtle and spare language, to offer a Christian alternative to Hegelian philosophy, though without mentioning the latter.[3] As the subtitle of the later work suggests, it does not contain a purely speculative attack against Hegel's grandiose world-historical system, but "an existential contribution" to the study of the self. Here Kierkegaard replaces the untenable spirit in Hegel's absolute idealism* with the category of the "single specific individual." The latter is an existential concept that remained at the heart of Kierkegaard's thought throughout his intellectual career.

The Sickness Unto Death appeared under the pseudonym Anti-Climacus in Copenhagen in 1849. By that time Kierkegaard was 36 years old and the book proved to be his penultimate major publication.[4] *The Sickness Unto Death* is a companion to Kierkegaard's earlier work *The Concept of Anxiety* (1844).[5] Whereas *The Concept of Anxiety* focuses more on the psychology of the self, *The Sickness Unto Death* is the product of Kierkegaard as a mature thinker, most interested in the religious stage of human existence. However, by writing under the pseudonym of Anti-Climacus, Kierkegaard wished to avoid appearing as a self-proclaimed authority with a definitive religious position. According to him, "Climacus has much in common with Anti-Climacus. But the difference is that while J. Climacus places himself so low that he even admits to not being a Christian, Anti-Climacus gives the impression of taking himself to be a Christian to an extraordinary degree ... I put myself higher than J. Climacus, lower than Anti-Climacus."[6]

The Sickness Unto Death was followed by *Practice in Christianity* (1850),[7] also published under the pseudonym Anti-Climacus. According to Alastair Hannay,* these two works form the underlying structure of the worldview expressed in the earlier pseudonymous writings. Moreover they are natural partners to the religious discourses among which they appeared (and more of which were to follow). *The Sickness Unto Death* resumes the theme of *The Concept of Anxiety* by Vigilius Haufniensis (another of Kierkegaard's pseudonyms); while *Practice in Christianity* resumes that of *Philosophical Fragments*.[8]

Integration

Even though Kierkegaard did not pursue a systemic approach to philosophy, his writings were not scattered or without overarching structure and purpose. There is indeed a parallel connection between the progression of the pseudonymous characters and the evolution of Kierkegaard's thought as a poet, a philosopher, a preacher, and finally a Christian. In this sense, Kierkegaard's pseudonymous authorship closely corresponds to his vision of the three stages of human existence. Accordingly, his pseudonymous publication begins with the "aesthetic" stage, namely "the immediate, the life of inclination, what comes naturally, the life of desire and aversion, of satisfaction and despair."[9] It then moves to the second stage, namely the "ethical stage" of a "life of commitment, task, of existential striving to actualize the vision of the good."[10] Finally it concludes in the "religious stage," namely "the life of receptivity, of gift and the expression of gratitude."[11] *The Sickness Unto Death* belongs to the latter category.

Kierkegaard's rationale for structuring his corpus in this way was based on his belief that, "If one is truly to succeed in leading a person to a specific place, one must first and foremost take care to find him where he is and begin there."[12] Thus each pseudonymous author characterizes a distinct stage of life where Kierkegaard assumes his readers to be. "Nevertheless, Kierkegaard insists that these widely contrasting works actually 'constitute stages in the realization of an idea.'"[13] Therefore, to understand Kierkegaard's overall philosophical project and his idea of the progression of the human self, it is very useful to consider his pseudonymous corpus as a whole.

Significance

The whole of Kierkegaard's philosophy and authorship was concerned with the essential question of "What it means to exist; … what it means to be a human being."[14] As mentioned above, Kierkegaard believes in three stages of life development and considers the religious stage to be the highest and most complete level of human existence. For him, one could become a true human self, a person, and an authentic individual only once one manages to reach the religious stage of existence. *The Sickness Unto Death* is therefore one of the most significant works in Kierkegaard's corpus. It is in this work that he offers his specific conception of the "theological self," meaning a self that is "conscious of being before God, by being a human self that has God as its standard."[15]

While it is true that Kierkegaard's therapeutic solution to the problem of despair is a Christian solution, it is not the case that in order to understand Kierkegaard or benefit from his work one has to be a believer in Christianity. His texts can benefit anyone with an open mind in terms of looking at the world differently—not from the narrow perspective of positivism.* *The Sickness Unto Death* provides profound psychological insights into the nature of human life, and what it means to be in despair and how to overcome it. In fact, some of the issues raised by Kierkegaard in his discussion of despair and anxiety—for example, his discussion of an alcoholic who loses his self or a young girl who despairs of love—are perhaps even more relevant today than they were in the early nineteenth century.[16]

NOTES

1   Typically Kierkegaard's *Edifying Discourses* invite "that single individual, my reader" to dwell with a biblical passage for the sake of building up faith. Kierkegaard published many of his *Edifying Discourses* in short collections to accompany particular pseudonymous texts, then later published them again in larger collections. See: William McDonald, "Søren Kierkegaard," in *The Stanford Encyclopedia of Philosophy* (Fall 2012), ed. Edward N. Zalta, autumn 2012, accessed July 31, 2015, http://plato.stanford.edu/archives/fall2012/entries/kierkegaard/.

2   Howard V. Hong and Edna H. Hong, eds., *The Essential Kierkegaard* (Princeton: Princeton University Press, 2000), ix.

3   See Alastair Hannay, in Søren Kierkegaard [Anti-Climacus, pseud.], *The Sickness Unto Death: A Christian Psychological Exposition for Edification and Awakening*, trans. Alastair Hannay (London: Penguin Classics, 1989), 29.

4   Alastair Hannay, in Kierkegaard, introduction to *Sickness Unto Death*, 26.

5   Søren Kierkegaard, *Kierkegaard's Writings, VIII: Concept of Anxiety: A Simple Psychologically Orienting Deliberation on the Dogmatic Issue of Hereditary Sin*, trans. Reidar Thomte (Princeton: Princeton University Press, 1981).

6   Quoted by Alastair Hannay, in Kierkegaard, introduction to *Sickness Unto Death*, 15.

7   Søren Kierkegaard, *Kierkegaard's Writings, XX: Practice in Christianity*, trans. Howard V. Hong and Edna H. Hong (Princeton: Princeton University Press, 1991).

8   In *Practice in Christianity*, he tried to reintroduce Christianity into "Christendom,"* a project that fully occupied him until his death. Kierkegaard accused the Church of Denmark of watering down the true message of Christianity and "Christendom," for promoting complacency and a "herd mentality" among bourgeois society. Alastair Hannay, in Kierkegaard, introduction to *Sickness Unto Death*, 30.

9   Howard V. Hong and Edna H. Hong, eds., *The Essential Kierkegaard* (Princeton: Princeton University Press, 2000), x.

10 Hong and Hong, *Essential Kierkegaard*, x.

11 Hong and Hong, *Essential Kierkegaard*, x.

12 Kierkegaard, *On My Work as an Author*, quoted in Hong and Hong, *Essential Kierkegaard*, x.

13 Kierkegaard, postscript, quoted in Mark C. Taylor, *Journeys to Selfhood: Hegel and Kierkegaard* (New York: Fordham University Press, 2000), 229.

14 Kierkegaard, postscript, quoted in Hong and Hong, *Essential Kierkegaard*, x.

15 Kierkegaard, *Sickness Unto Death*, 111.

16 Kierkegaard, *Sickness Unto Death*, 50, 142–3.

SECTION 3
IMPACT

THE FIRST RESPONSES

KEY POINTS

- Kierkegaard was deeply offended by the *ad hominem** attacks launched against him by the satirical journal *The Corsair.**

- He waited until the death of his father and their family friend and priest Bishop Mynster before he published his most direct critique of "Christendom."*

- Kierkegaard's works did not have any significant short-term impact on the state of theology and philosophy in Denmark; however, they significantly influenced the next generation of philosophers and theologians and set the stage for the emergence of existentialism* as one of the most influential schools of thought in the twentieth century.

Criticism

A few years before *The Sickness Unto Death: A Christian Psychological Exposition of Edification and Awakening*, Søren Kierkegaard published his first major work, *Either/Or* (1843). The text at once inspired a lively controversy in Copenhagen, both in private discussions and in the press, and was given an understanding and friendly reception, even by the cool J. L. Heiberg* and the revolutionary M. A. Goldschmidt.* The latter's review in *The Corsair* was perhaps the most positive the satirical magazine ever published."[1]

Aside from this, the quality and integrity of the criticisms leveled against Kierkegaard were far removed from the standard of his own work. Perhaps one controversial incident in his life best illustrates this point, namely *The Corsair* affair. As this episode had a major impact on

> **❝ I would rather be a swine-herd out on Amager and be understood by swine than be a poet and be misunderstood by people. ❞**
> Søren Kierkegaard, *Either/Or*

Kierkegaard and features in every biography of him, it merits attention here.

In 1845 the literary critic P. L. Møller* wrote a disparaging, though anonymous, review of Kierkegaard's *Stages on Life's Way* (1845)[2] in *The Corsair*. Møller described the book as extremely "hysterical in its masochistic tendencies as to border on madness"; moreover, "he gave the reader more than a hint that Kierkegaard had inconsiderably used his fiancée [Regine Olsen*] as a model and exposed the private tragedy of their love affair to the public gaze."[3] Kierkegaard was deeply upset and angered by the critics' lack of understanding, especially given the several years of hard work that had gone into writing the book. In response he wrote an article in the daily newspaper *The Fatherland* (*Fædrelandet*; December 27, 1845), which crushed Møller's reputation once and for all. Kierkegaard revealed Møller's identity as a regular contributor to the academically disreputable journal *The Corsair*, something that hitherto had been a secret. This revelation had a deadly effect on Møller's career. The writer left Denmark* and never fulfilled his academic ambitions. However, this did not mark the end of *The Corsair* affair. The journal's young editor, M. A. Goldschmidt, went on to launch an *ad hominem* smear campaign against Kierkegaard, featuring demeaning caricatures of him (drawn by the Danish caricaturist P. C. Klæstrup*), mocking his appearance, mainly his slightly deformed posture, the umbrella that he always carried, and especially his asymmetric trousers.

Outside the press and so far as the contemporary debate goes, Kierkegaard's work did not receive any substantial critique from other

theologians and philosophers. The primate bishop H. L. Martensen*
was quite concerned with his activities and opposition to the State
Church of Denmark but did not openly challenge him. Kierkegaard's
family friend and priest, Bishop Mynster (who preceded Martensen),
was also critical of Kierkegaard's antagonistic stance vis-à-vis the State
Church but often kept silent or resorted to indirect criticism—for
example, by praising the work of Kierkegaard's rivals. It was only
decades after his death in 1855 that Kierkegaard's works started to be
really intellectually appraised.

Responses

The Corsair affair was the most brutal attack that Kierkegaard
experienced during his lifetime. "His contempt for the vulgarity he
met with from the public impelled him to a self-assertion psychopathic
in character."[4] He even began to employ the term "brutality" in his
work to describe the public's savagery, devoid of ideas: "He had talked
to people about their souls' eternal salvation and they thanked him by
making jests about his trousers."[5]

   Despite their intellectual emptiness, these kinds of brutal *ad
hominem* attacks had an effect on Kierkegaard. Although they did not
compel him to revise his arguments about the nature of human beings,
they made him feel more and more isolated and beyond the intellectual
capacities of his own era. He clearly stated his feelings about the
public's reaction to his work, especially with reference to *The Corsair*
affair, in a journal entry as follows: "So it continues [that is, the public's
mockery of him], and when I am dead people's eyes will be opened,
they will marvel at what I have desired, at the same time behaving in
the same way to someone else, who is probably the only man who
understands me. … God in heaven, if there were not deep within a
man a place where all this can be completely forgotten in communion
with Thee, who could endure it?"[6]

Conflict and Consensus

The Sickness Unto Death was Kierkegaard's penultimate major publication. In this work and in his final major publication, *Practice in Christianity* (1850),[7] he articulated his most comprehensive religious conception of the human self and provided a thorough critique of the state of the individual within "Christendom." However, he refrained from publishing his most uncompromisingly direct critique of the established order and the State Church, contained in *Judge for Yourself!*[8] He did so out of respect for Bishop Mynster and because he thought that Mynster would soon agree that Christianity was being depleted of its true meaning in "Christendom."[9] However, Mynster never admitted to such a belief and Kierkegaard decided to wait until the bishop's death in 1854 before publishing his most direct critique of the State Church. These appeared in various articles published in *The Fatherland* (*Fædrelandet*) newspaper, as well as in a series of pamphlets that he personally published under the title of *The Moment* (Øjeblikket, 1855).[10]

This suggests that not only did Kierkegaard fail to modify his views of the State Church, but he in fact increased the directness of his critique toward the end of his life. He maintained a "characteristic sense of humor" in the series of writings during his last year of life "but in the keenly sharpened form of hard-hitting criticism, at times, caustic caricature. An authorship that began as indirect communication ended as direct."[11]

Kierkegaard's contemporary critics did not modify their views of his work and of the established order either. In fact, both "Christendom" and Hegelianism* lost their influence in Denmark gradually over the years, though not as a result of and not under any direct influence from Kierkegaard's works. His texts had little effect on the popularity of Hegelianism partly due to Martensen.* Martensen, a staunch Hegelian theologian, succeeded Mynster as the bishop primate of the Danish Church. He ensured that Hegelianism remained the most influential school of thought in Denmark during his time.

Despite their short-term failure in influencing the critics or the established order in theology and philosophy, Kierkegaard's writings had a significant impact on the next generation of philosophers and theologians, especially in the twentieth century.

NOTES

1   Peter Rohde, *Søren Kierkegaard: An Introduction to His Life and Philosophy*, trans. Alan Moray Williams (London: Allen & Unwin, 1963), 89, 112.

2   Søren Kierkegaard, *Kierkegaard's Writings, XI: Stages on Life's Way*, eds. Howard V. Hong and Edna H. Hong (Princeton: Princeton University Press, 2013).

3   Rohde, *Søren Kierkegaard*, 114.

4   Rohde, *Søren Kierkegaard*, 119.

5   Rohde, *Søren Kierkegaard*, 119.

6   Quoted in Rohde, *Søren Kierkegaard*, 120.

7   Søren Kierkegaard, *Kierkegaard's Writings, XX: Practice in Christianity*, trans. Howard V. Hong and Edna H. Hong (Princeton: Princeton University Press, 1991).

8   This work is now published as part of Kierkegaard's "Writings" collection; see: Søren Kierkegaard, *Kierkegaard's Writings, XXI: For Self-Examination/ Judge for Yourself!*, eds. Howard V. Hong and Edna H. Hong (Princeton: Princeton University Press, 1991).

9   Howard V. Hong and Edna H. Hong, eds., *The Essential Kierkegaard* (Princeton: Princeton University Press, 2000), 424.

10 Søren Kierkegaard, *The Moment and Late Writings: Kierkegaard's Writings, Vol. 23*, trans. Howard V. Hong and Edna H. Hong (Princeton: Princeton University Press, 1998). These pamphlets are now also included in Søren Kierkegaard and H. A. Johnson, *Attack Upon Christendom*, trans. Walter Macon Lowrie (Princeton: Princeton University Press, 1968).

11 Hong and Hong, *Essential Kierkegaard*, 424.

THE EVOLVING DEBATE

KEY POINTS

- Kierkegaard's emphasis on the "single specific individual" as the main unit of analysis and his anti-systemic approach to philosophy set the stage for the emergence of existentialism* in the twentieth century. However, most twentieth-century existentialist thinkers developed an atheistic version of Kierkegaard's Christian insights.

- Kierkegaard is often considered the father of existentialism because he was the first to dedicate the whole of his philosophy to a discussion of the single specific individual and his or her real-life concerns such as despair, anxiety, angst, responsibility, freedom, and death.

- His religious writings, key among them *The Sickness Unto Death,* deeply influenced the state of theology and set the stage for the emergence of an existential approach to religion in the twentieth and twenty-first centuries.

Uses and Problems

Søren Kierkegaard's realization of the limited powers of the intellect to answer the ultimate questions of life has continued to preoccupy modern thought.[1] On the one hand, his subjective and individualist approach to psychology and philosophy, especially as it is presented in *The Sickness Unto Death:A Christian Psychological Exposition of Edification and Awakening,* continues to have a profound impact on the evolution of these fields in the twentieth century. Kierkegaard's individualism found its most distinctive expression in the philosophical school of thought known as existentialism, which permeated the intellectual

> ❝ There can be no doubt that most of the thinkers who are usually associated with the existentialist tradition, for whatever their actual doctrines, were in one way or another influenced by the writings of Kierkegaard. [On the other hand] it was with existentialism that Kierkegaard first entered the standard canon of Western philosophy. From that point on it has been customary to begin introductory courses on existentialism with a lecture on Kierkegaard or to include a snippet from his works in anthologies of existentialist thinkers. ❞
>
> Jon Bartley Stewart, *Kierkegaard and Existentialism*

environment of postwar Europe. On the other, *The Sickness Unto Death* had a lasting impact on the subsequent evolution of theology as an academic field of inquiry that has God as its main subject—as opposed to psychology, for example, that places human beings at its center.

Kierkegaard's theology opened up a new field of faith-based inquiry. Robert L. Perkins suggests that "not since Augustine's *Confessions* or Pascal's *Pensées* have we confronted so full and thorough an analysis of the human subject in its relationship to itself and to grace. ...The whole theological discussion of dialogue in the twentieth century, though emphasised by numerous writers, owes much to the fundamental and radical Kierkegaardian interpretation of the divine–human encounter."[2] Kierkegaard's subjective approach, his emphasis on the primacy of action vis-à-vis pure thought, and the primacy of the single specific individual in relation to the abstract or the positivistic* conception of the human race, helped set the stage for the emergence of an existential approach to religion in the twentieth and twenty-first centuries.[3]

Schools of Thought

Kierkegaard is often considered the father of existentialism. He was the first to dedicate the whole of his philosophy to the individual and his or her concerns with despair, anxiety, responsibility, death, and faith. However, contemporary existentialism's association with atheism turned Kierkegaard's thought upside down. Whereas the core of Kierkegaard's existentialism was Christian faith, the most prominent existentialist thinkers of the twentieth century, notably Martin Heidegger,* Jean-Paul Sartre,* and Albert Camus,* rejected the idea of a divine Creator and declared the individual to be alone in the world, rather than standing alone "before God."

Heidegger's existential categories in his most influential book, *Being and Time* (1927),[4] were influenced by Kierkegaard's writings, although this was not explicitly acknowledged by Heidegger. Moreover, Heidegger did not remain faithful to Kierkegaard's theistic approach: "God, who, for Kierkegaard, is the beginning and the end of any Christian's ontological questioning, is bracketed by Heidegger as a merely 'ontic'* concern."[5]   Heidegger was also influenced by Friedrich Nietzsche's* "death of God" philosophy, another nineteenth-century philosophy that is now often discussed under the category of existentialism.

In the twentieth century, Sartre offered a third version of atheistic existentialism. Sartre's existentialism was "structurally the most faithful to Kierkegaard's philosophical position. Unlike Heidegger, Sartre engages explicitly and positively with Kierkegaard's writing."[6] Nevertheless, Sartre's discussion of the self, as an ungrounded center of freedom, opposes Kierkegaard's central statement in *The Sickness Unto Death* that the self can cure itself from despair only by grounding itself "transparently in the power that established it," that is, in God.[7]

Kierkegaard's conception of the self is a synthesis between three sets of dialectical relationships: finite and infinite, temporal and eternal, and freedom and necessity. He emphasizes that for God everything is possible and that belief in this axiom is what defines faith. In other words, to have faith is to believe that for God everything is possible.[8] For Sartre, by contrast, the self was not a synthesis. For him, the fundamental nature of human existence is to be a consciousness that is irreducibly for itself. By this, Sartre means a consciousness capable of self-awareness, and so always capable of having some understanding of what it is doing. Insofar as we are free to determine our own course of action through our choices, we are ultimately responsible for our own lives.[9] For Sartre, a human being seeks to become God, and only in being a God would his or her contradictions fully resolve. In contrast, for Kierkegaard, wanting to become God is viewed as an active form of despair and as sinful.

Sartre's seminal work *Being and Nothingness* (1943)[10] and his essay "The Humanism of Existentialism" (1946), show "what happens to a Kierkegaardian individual who is disconnected from God: the absence of grounds for his existence ('nothingness') is a brute fact that reveals that life is absurd, in either a comic or a tragic sense."[11]

In the final analysis, the atheistic conception of freedom is far removed from Kierkegaard's Christian conception of it. In an ironic way, Sartre's existentialism provides the exact opposite of Kierkegaard's existentialist philosophy. However, they both focus on the single specific individual and his or her universally human concerns.

In Current Scholarship

Kierkegaard's *Sickness Unto Death* has had a significant and lasting impact on a diverse range of academic fields.[12] Besides its immediate impact on the evolution of anti-systemic approaches to philosophy and Christian theology, it has also influenced the evolution of modern psychology.

In *The Birth and Death of Meaning*,[13] the cultural anthropologist Ernest Becker* refers to Kierkegaard as "one of the greatest modern theorists of anxiety."[14] Becker's own work was influenced by

Kierkegaard's thought, especially his *The Denial of Death* (1973).[15] The German psychoanalyst and social psychologist Erich Fromm* has also emphasized Kierkegaard's lasting influence and his efforts to maximize individuality among his contemporary as well as future readers.[16]

Kierkegaard's notion of the absurd has reappeared in art and literature, especially in the postwar period in Europe. A broad range of writers who engaged with existentialist themes such as despair, anxiety, and suicide looked to Kierkegaard for insight. Among these are Franz Kafka,* the literary critic and philosopher György Lukács,* and, perhaps most prominently, Albert Camus.[17] However, despite being influenced by Kierkegaard's works, these thinkers secularized Kierkegaard's religious idea of human existence and offered their own atheistic explanation of his existentialist categories.

NOTES

1   Peter Rohde, *Søren Kierkegaard: An Introduction to His Life and Philosophy*, trans. Alan Moray Williams (London: Allen & Unwin, 1963), 149.

2   Robert L. Perkins, *Søren Kierkegaard* (London: Lutterworth Press, 1969), 44.

3   In the twentieth century, for example, the existential approach to religion was developed by a diverse range of theologians and religious thinkers including Gabriel Marcel (1889–1973), Nicholas Berdyaev (1874–1948), Paul Tillich (1886–1965), Rudolf Bultmann (1884–1976), Miguel de Unamuno (1865–1936), Lev Shestov (1865–1938), Karl Barth (1886–1968), and Martin Buber (1878–1965). See: Hubert L. Dreyfus and Mark A. Wrathall, *A Companion to Phenomenology and Existentialism* (Chichester: John Wiley & Sons, 2011), 4. For a study of "religious existentialism" see: Clancy Martin, "Religious Existentialism," in *A Companion*, Dreyfus and Wrathall, 118–205.

4   Martin Heidegger, *Being and Time*, trans. J. Macquarrie and E. Robinson (Oxford: Basil Blackwell, 1962).

5   Clare Carlisle, *Kierkegaard's Philosophy of Becoming: Movements and Positions* (New York: State University of New York Press, 2005), 140.

6   Carlisle, *Kierkegaard's Philosophy of Becoming*, 144.

7   Søren Kierkegaard [Anti-Climacus, pseud.], *The Sickness Unto Death: A Christian Psychological Exposition for Edification and Awakening*, trans. Alastair Hannay (London: Penguin Books, 1989), 44.

8   Kierkegaard, *Sickness Unto Death*, 68.

9   Charles Guignon, ed., *The Existentialists: Critical Essays on Kierkegaard, Nietzsche, Heidegger, and Sartre* (Lanham, MD: Rowman & Littlefield, 2004), 13.

10   Jean-Paul Sartre, *Being and Nothingness*, trans. Hazel E. Barnes (New York: Washington Square Press, 1993).

11   Carlisle, *Kierkegaard's Philosophy of Becoming*, 144.

12   For a comprehensive account of Kierkegaard's influence on the social sciences see: Jon Bartley Stewart, ed., *Kierkegaard's Influence on the Social Sciences*, Kierkegaard Research: Sources, Reception and Resources, Vol. 13 (Farnham: Ashgate Publishing, 2011).

13   Ernest Becker, *The Birth and Death of Meaning: An Interdisciplinary Perspective on the Problem of Man* (New York: Free Press, 1971).

14   Ernest Becker, quoted in Rick Anthony Furtak, "Ernest Becker: A Kierkegaardian Theorist of Death and Human Nature," in *Kierkegaard's Influence on the Social Sciences*, ed. Stewart, 19.

15   Ernest Becker, *The Denial of Death* (New York: Free Press, 1997).

16   See, for example: John Lippitt's discussion of the relationship between Fromm and Kierkegaard in his chapter on "Eric Fromm: The Integrity of the Self and the Practice of Love," in *Kierkegaard's Influence on the Social Sciences*, ed. Stewart, 95–119.

17   Hubert L. Dreyfus and Mark A. Wrathall, "A Brief Introduction to Phenomenology and Existentialism", in *A Companion*, Dreyfus and Wrathall, 4–5.

IMPACT AND INFLUENCE TODAY

KEY POINTS

- Because of its emphasis on the real and universal issues of human concern, such as despair and anxiety, Kierkegaard's *Sickness Unto Death* remains relevant today.

- Kierkegaard's anti-systemic and "unscientific" approach to the problem of despair continues to challenge positivistic* and disinterested approaches to psychology.

- Despite being deeply influenced by Kierkegaard's works, most of the existentialist* thinkers of the twentieth century secularized Kierkegaard's ideas and offered their own atheistic explanation of Kierkegaard's existentialist categories.

Position

Søren Kierkegaard's works, especially *The Sickness Unto Death: A Christian Psychological Exposition of Edification and Awakening*, mark the beginning of one of the most significant recent attempts "in the history of philosophy to foreground the practical problems of living, to relate these to the historical conditions of modernity, and to think [about] them in a way that is both philosophically sophisticated and practically concrete. It is this connection of philosophical reflection to the problems of life as it is lived in the contemporary world" that explains why existentialism in general and Kierkegaard's works in particular remain appealing, relevant, and still thought-provoking today.[1]

Kierkegaard's *Sickness Unto Death* in particular continues to challenge modern behavioral psychology and its proclaimed objective

> ** 66 ** Kierkegaard's works, written over a century ago in a minor language, have been rediscovered throughout the world because they speak to the human condition, especially in a period that is an exacerbated continuation of what Kierkegaard called … 'an age of moral disintegration. ** 99 **
>
> Howard V. Hong and Edna H. Hong, *The Essential Kierkegaard*

and disinterested approach to universally human concerns such as despair, anxiety, death, and suicide. With its definition of the self as a synthesis between the finite and the infinite, the temporal and the eternal, the text questions the atheist and nihilistic trends in philosophy, sociology, and psychology that deny any relationship between man and God, or even the existence of God altogether. Kierkegaard's work brings back the eternal into the understanding of the human self and provides an alternative analysis and solution of modernity's peculiar problems.

In addition to its philosophical account of the individual human self, *The Sickness Unto Death* also provides a thorough critique of an entire epoch. The author constantly encourages his readers to first become aware of themselves (self-awareness), especially of the self's relationship with the "power that has established it"—God. He then motivates his readers to become aware of their "present age." Finally, he inspires his readers to criticize the complacency and "herd mentality" of the present age, in terms of religious or cultural activities and in terms of philosophical systemization and abstraction of the world. *The Sickness Unto Death* therefore continues to "be read as one of the most incisive contributions to a critique of modernity. In this respect it confirms, completes, and anticipates analyses written by Karl Marx,* Friedrich Nietzsche,* and Sigmund Freud."*[2]

Interaction

Even though Kierkegaard's writings deeply influenced existentialist thinkers of the twentieth century, most of these thinkers in fact provided a secularized, if not always atheistic, conception of the human self. In doing so they radically transformed Kierkegaard's Christian approach to the problem of despair and anxiety. It is of course impossible to know what Kierkegaard's reaction would have been to such an inversion of his essentially Christian thought. It is not hard to imagine that these developments would not have come as a surprise to him, mainly because of his belief that every age is assigned the task of becoming anew and no one can learn how to achieve selfhood from the previous generation. With regard to different disciplines, such as theology, philosophy, and psychology, he also believed that they are tasked with recreating their categories relevant to the needs and concerns of their own "present age." Accordingly, Kierkegaard would not have been surprised to learn that the future generations of writers and philosophers have arrived at a different definition of selfhood, one that is radically different from his Christian understanding of the human self. Whether he would have approved of the new conception of the human self is altogether a different question.

The Continuing Debate

Regardless of the atheistic nature of their thought, the twentieth-century existentialist thinkers, such as Jean-Paul Sartre,* Martin Heidegger,* and Albert Camus,* employed Kierkegaard's concept of the single specific individual as a powerful starting point for thinking about the human condition. They further expanded the notion of the absurd, though often devoid of its religious associations, and reformulated the paradox of the human being as an entity that is left in between its eternal/infinite aspirations and its temporal/finite conditionality in this world.

Today, however, in the globalized world of the early twenty-first century—dominated by capitalism,* consumerism,* neoliberal policies, and mass culture—the public has increasingly become distanced from the popular existentialist trend of the twentieth century. It has been argued that existentialism in its *cultural* manifestation "was distinctively a phenomenon of the mid-twentieth century" and as such "*is* outmoded" today.[3]

This is not to say that the concerns raised by Kierkegaard in *The Sickness Unto Death*, and later by Sartre in *Being and Nothingness* (1943),[4] and by Camus in *The Rebel* (1951)[5] have been resolved or even partially answered. Today's world is still occupied with questions of despair, anxiety, suicide, and the meaning of life, perhaps even more than ever before. The global economic crisis, the personality stereotypes promoted by live reality shows around the world, and other conditions of life in the early twenty-first century have been influential in bringing about a lack of genuine selfhood and thus, arguably, a deepening of a fundamental despair. As a result, people of the twenty-first century, especially artists, writers, and poets, are engaging more and more with these existential themes; however, this does not imply any direct or conscious engagement with Kierkegaard's writings. Moreover, given the secularized state of social sciences and humanities in the West, especially psychology, it would not be accurate to suggest that Kierkegaard's faith-based response to the question of human despair permeates everyday life in the contemporary era, nor that it is appreciated by the general public.

NOTES

1   Felicity Joseph, Jack Reynolds, and Ashley Woodward, *The Bloomsbury Companion to Existentialism* (London: Bloomsbury Publishing, 2014), 3.

2   Louis K. Dupré, "*The Sickness Unto Death*: Critique of the Modern Age," in *The Existentialists: Critical Essays on Kierkegaard, Nietzsche, Heidegger, and Sartre*, ed. Charles Guignon (Lanham: MD: Rowman & Littlefield, 2004), 49–50.

3   Joseph, Reynolds, and Woodward, *Bloomsbury Companion*, 2.

4   Jean-Paul Sartre, *Being and Nothingness*, trans. Hazel E. Barnes (New York: Washington Square Press, 1993).

5   Albert Camus, *The Rebel: An Essay on Man in Revolt* (New York: Vintage, 1992).

MODULE 12
WHERE NEXT?

KEY POINTS

- *The Sickness Unto Death* will most likely continue to be used as an example of a comprehensive intellectual inquiry into the nature of human self from an existentialist* perspective.

- Kierkegaard's untiring emphasis on "the single specific individual" and the realm of "lived human experience" ensures that his writings will continue to be relevant in the future.

- *The Sickness Unto Death* is representative of Kierkegaard's theological, philosophical, psychological, and literary writings. Moreover, it marks the emergence of the "single specific individual" as a main unit of analysis in philosophy. It is therefore a seminal text in philosophy.

Potential

The continued influence of Kierkegaard's work consists in his struggle against the academic tendency toward "disinterested" analysis of the world and spiritlessness. *The Sickness Unto Death: A Christian Psychological Exposition of Edification and Awakening*, like all of Kierkegaard's other works, envisions "the possibility of a renewal in which individuals recover from their dispirited state and come to live as individuals with the passion and intensity that is characteristic of fully realized human existence."[1] Even though Kierkegaard's ideas and solutions, especially the central issue of despair, "is cast in religious terms, it can help us understand the possibility of self-fulfilment and the achievement of intensity ('spirit') in life through non-religious forms of commitment."[2]

> ❝ Kierkegaard wrote for 'that individual,' and through time he has in fact been read by 'that individual,' and remains important for those making an individual, dissonant, or even subversive, contribution to their own subject. Official, academic philosophy does not have much use for him, is given to denying him philosophical status, and quite often raises the question as to whether he is even of any philosophical interest. And all this is exactly the way Kierkegaard would have wanted it. ❞
>
> Roger Poole, *The Cambridge Companion to Kierkegaard*

The Sickness Unto Death will most likely continue to be used as an example of a comprehensive intellectual inquiry into the nature of the human self and its concerns from a subjective, non-scientific, and "interested" (that is, passionate) perspective. Kierkegaard's approach serves as a model for an alternative methodology to deal with inherently human questions of anxiety and despair. Regardless of his religious conclusions, Kierkegaard's methodology and existentialist categories are useful and enlightening. As long as humanity's state of despair persists, and as long as the anxiety of the single specific individual lingers, Kierkegaard's *Sickness Unto Death* is likely to remain a relevant and indeed a useful source in addressing, framing, and potentially tackling such issues.

Future Directions

One aspect of Kierkegaard's work that ensures its continuous influence is its emphasis on the realm of "lived human experience." Today an increasing number of scholars in various disciplines are directing their attention to the domain of the individual and his or her experience. This is true in, for example, the field of oral history (as compared to the conventional state-centered historiography). Feminism and various new directives in other realms of the humanities and social sciences have also begun to champion the primacy of lived human experience in their analyses of sociopolitical and cultural phenomena.[3]

Another inspiring aspect of Kierkegaard's thought "arises from his profound spirituality, coupled with an ability to address undogmatically [that is, with an open mind] a multiplicity of interests and interest groups ... attracting the interest of vastly different disciplines, from religious studies to computer studies and psychics."[4] Kierkegaard's use of the Socratic* indirect method of communication, especially through his pseudonymous writings, is another stimulating aspect of his work. According to one of Kierkegaard's leading commentators, "it is this feature of Kierkegaard's writing that makes him especially effective in a time when two main tendencies seem to be especially dominant—a pluralism that accepts the personal validity of all views but stands by the correctness of no particular view of the universe, and a scientific or religious fundamentalism that is rigidly exclusive of views other than its own. Kierkegaard avoids the pitfalls of both trends, and he also does something else; he makes room for truth, both intellectual and existential."[5]

Summary

Kierkegaard's aim in *The Sickness Unto Death* is to explain the problem of human despair by providing a new conception of the self as consisting of a relationship between opposing factors. He believes that despair occurs when the balance between these opposing factors is upset. He then attempts to provide a remedy to the universal problem of despair. He finds this solution in (Christian) faith and the belief that the human being, in relating to itself, stands alone before God and that for God anything is possible. Therefore, one should not despair.

The Sickness Unto Death is a key text in the author's substantial body of work. It is representative of Kierkegaard's theological, philosophical, psychological, and literary writings and therefore deserves special attention from anyone who is interested in the genesis of the concept of the "single specific individual" and the existentialist understanding of the human self as opposed to the abstract and idealist or positivistic conceptions of the self. Moreover, it contains the origins of the existential movement in psychology and the introduction of phenomenology* to psychiatry. (This movement is particularly related to the emergence of existential psychotherapy, a unique style of therapy that puts emphasis on the human condition as a whole.) Therefore, the text is considered seminal and will most likely continue to be considered as such.

Although Kierkegaard speaks extensively about the incompatibility between reason and faith (what he called the "paradox of Christianity"), he is not an irrationalist. He tries to clarify the diversity of different forms of knowing and different levels of human experience and the multifaceted nature of human existence. He opposes monolithic accounts of human existence, whether those that proclaim the role of reason (for example Kant's* and Hegel's*) as the most important aspect of existence, or those that promote, even if unknowingly, a "herd mentality" which is accompanied by a lack of individual responsibility in matters of faith (that is, mainstream theologians and the clergy). He criticized both of these trends in his work, a critique that applies to the state of scholarship and religion in today's world as much as it did to Denmark* of the early nineteenth century.

NOTES

1   Charles Guignon, ed., *The Existentialists: Critical Essays on Kierkegaard, Nietzsche, Heidegger, and Sartre* (Lanham, MD: Rowman & Littlefield, 2004), 5.

2   Guignon, *Existentialists*, 5.

3   See in particular: Jon Bartley Stewart, ed., *Kierkegaard and Existentialism* (Farnham: Ashgate Publishing, 2011); and the collection of essays in "Part II – New Direction," in *The Bloomsbury Companion to Existentialism*,

Felicity Joseph, Jack Reynolds, and Ashley Woodward (London: Bloomsbury Publishing, 2014).

4   Julia Watkin, *Kierkegaard* (London: Geoffrey Chapman, 1997), 107.

5   Watkin, *Kierkegaard*, 108.

GLOSSARY

GLOSSARY OF TERMS

Absolute Idealism/German idealism: philosophical system associated principally with G. W. F. Hegel. It proposes that the finite world is a reflection of the mind, that the only way for human beings to know the world is through pure thought, and that only the conscious mind is real. Without conscious thought, we would have no way of accessing the word and have no certainty about our knowledge of the world.

Ad hominem: name of a fallacy, that is, an incorrect form of reasoning. The mistake made in an *ad hominem* argument is that one attacks the person rather than the ideas. *Ad hominem* literally means "to the person."

Bourgeoisie: social order made up of the middle classes. In social and political theory, the term is used by Marxists to describe the social class that monopolizes the benefits of modernization in detriment of the proletariat.

Capitalism: an economic system based on private ownership, private enterprise, and the maximization of profit.

Christendom (*Christenheden* in Danish): for Kierkegaard, Christendom is official Christianity. This is separate from the Christianity of the New Testament, and works as an expression of the institutional values of Christianity by churchgoers who do not necessarily live their lives according to the values of the New Testament.

Consumerism: set of beliefs within a society that emphasizes the acquisition of consumer goods as the basis for economic growth.

The Corsair: Danish weekly satirical magazine, published by Meïr Aron Goldschmidt. The magazine was published between 1840 and 1846.

Dialectics: process especially associated with Hegel of arriving at the truth by stating a thesis, developing a contradictory antithesis, and combining and resolving them into a coherent synthesis.

Enlightenment: period in European history from the early seventeenth to the late eighteenth century. This period was characterized by a deep distrust of religious authority, especially that of the Catholic Church, and any reliance on tradition. Instead, it emphasized reason, critical analysis, and the importance of each individual.

Existentialism: term used to describe a complex philosophical tradition emerging in the 1930s with many forms and varieties. Broadly, it can be said to focus philosophy on human existence in the world, and on the possibilities available to human beings in the world. Key existential philosophers include Jean-Paul Sartre, Simone de Beauvoir, and Albert Camus.

Feudal order: dominant social system in Europe during the Middle Ages. In practice, feudalism meant that a country was not governed by a king but by individual members of the nobility who administered their own estates, dispensed justice, and levied taxes. The nobility held lands from the Crown in exchange for military service, while vassals and peasants were obliged to contribute to the nobility's wealth in exchange for military protection.

Hegelianism (see also **Absolute idealism**): philosophy that developed from the ideas of G. W. F. Hegel. This can be summed up by how Hegel places reality in ideas and thought, rather than in things, and the ways in which he uses dialectic to understand the ideas behind all phenomena.

Metaphysics: branch of philosophy concerned with explaining the nature of being. Metaphysics investigates both what there is and what it is like. It attempts to clarify fundamental notions such as space and time, objects and properties, cause and effect, and possibilities. Ontic: technical term employed by Martin Heidegger. Ontic refers to particular entities and the facts about them. Heidegger opposes the ontic to the ontological, the latter being a more fundamental account of the being of particular entities.

Phenomenology: study of the structures of human consciousness. The phenomenological movement is an influential twentieth- and twenty-first-century philosophical tradition. Leading figures other than Edmund Husserl include the German philosopher Martin Heidegger, the French philosopher Maurice Merleau-Ponty, and the French existentialist philosopher Jean-Paul Sartre.

Positivism: philosophical system elaborated from the 1830s by the French thinker Auguste Comte. Positivism recognizes only the empirical data of experience, such as observable phenomena or scientific laws, and excludes *a priori* conclusions or metaphysical speculations.

Principle of non-contradiction: logical principle which holds that two conflicting (contradictory) propositions cannot be true at the same time. The principle was first discussed by Aristotle in his book on *Metaphysics* IV (Gamma).

Pseudonym: a fictitious name, usually used by an author.

World spirit (*Weltgeist*): Hegelian concept, which refers to the spirit that defines and makes real any particular epoch.

World War II (1939–45): the most widespread military conflict in history, resulting in more than 50 million casualties. While the conflict began with Germany's invasion of Poland in 1939, it soon involved all of the major world powers, who gradually formed two military alliances and were eventually joined by a great number of the world's nations.

PEOPLE MENTIONED IN THE TEXT

Aristotle (384–322 B.C.E.) was a Greek polymath and philosopher who studied under Plato. Although he is now remembered primarily for his ethics and political theory, Aristotle also wrote important works on diverse subjects such as tragedy, rhetoric, and biology.

Ernest Becker (1924–74) was a Jewish-American cultural anthropologist and author known for his 1974 Pulitzer Prize-winning book, *The Denial of Death*.

Albert Camus (1913–60) was a French novelist, existentialist philosopher, and journalist, who was awarded the Nobel Prize in Literature in 1957.

Sigmund Freud (1856–1939) was an Austrian neurologist and the founder of psychoanalysis. He proposed that a system of unconscious drives and repressions determined much of human behavior.

Erich Fromm (1900–80) was a German psychologist and humanist philosopher. He is known for developing a concept of freedom that is an intrinsic part of human nature.

M. A. Goldschmidt (1819–87) was a Danish publisher, editor, and novelist.

N. F. S. Grundtvig (1783–1872) was a Danish theologian, pastor, educator, and poet who, unlike Kierkegaard, had emphasized the light, communal, and celebratory aspects of Christianity.

Alastair Hannay (b. 1932) is emeritus professor in philosophy at the University of Oslo. He has translated works by Kierkegaard, written a (2003) biography about him, and published a (1999) book on Kierkegaard's philosophy entitled *Kierkegaard*.

Georg Wilhelm Friedrich Hegel (1770–1831) was a German idealist philosopher. He became well known for his historicist and realist accounts of reality, and his concept of a "system" of integration between mind and nature, subject and object, was one of the first conceptual moves that acknowledged contradictions and oppositions within such a system.

J. L. Heiberg (1791–1860) was a Danish poet and critic. He is known for his Hegelian philosophy and for his contributions to the Romantic movement in Denmark.

Martin Heidegger (1889–1976) was a controversial German philosopher. His magnum opus, *Being and Time* (1927), dedicated to his teacher Edmund Husserl, is thought to be one of the central works of the phenomenological movement.

David Hume (1711–76) was a Scottish philosopher, historian, and essayist who was known for his extreme skepticism, his religious agnosticism, and his impartiality.

Franz Kafka (1883–1924) was a Jewish German-language novelist and writer of short stories, who lived in Prague; he is best known for his complex parables of subjugated human existence, including *The Trial*, published posthumously in 1925.

Immanuel Kant (1724–1804) was a German philosopher,

considered today to be among the founders of modern philosophy. He is best known for his *Critique of Pure Reason* (1781), in which he argues regarding the limits of reason in understanding human experience.

Michael P. Kierkegaard (1756–1838) was Søren Kierkegaard's father.

P. C. Klæstrup (1820–82) was a well-known Danish caricaturist.

György Lukács (1885–1971) was a Hungarian Marxist philosopher, who made important contributions to Marxism in the first half of the twentieth century.

Gabriel Marcel (1889–1973) was a French philosopher, dramatist, and critic, usually regarded as the first French existential philosopher. He is also known for having coined the term "existentialism" in a 1943 review of Jean-Paul Sartre's *Being and Nothingness*.

H. L. Martensen (1808–84) was a Hegelian professor of theology at Copenhagen University who later became the bishop primate of the Danish Church.

Karl Marx (1818–83) was a German sociologist, economist, and revolutionary. Along with Friedrich Engels he wrote *The Communist Manifesto* and *Das Kapital*, which form the basis of the body of thought known as Marxism.

P. L. Møller (1814–65) was a Danish literary critic.

P. M. Møller (1794–1838) was a Danish writer, philosopher, and academic, best known for his friendship with Kierkegaard.

J. P. Mynster (1775–1854) was a Danish theologian and bishop of Zealand, Denmark, from 1834 until his death. He was also Kierkegaard's family friend and priest.

Friedrich Nietzsche (1844–1900) was a widely influential German philologist and philosopher. Against the largely Christian leanings of his age, Nietzsche was known for looking up to a Greek ethic that privileged honor and power.

Regine Olsen (1822–1904) was Søren Kierkegaard's former fiancée.

Jean-Paul Sartre (1905–80) was a leading French existential philosopher, writer, and activist. His work relied heavily on the idea that individuals are condemned to be free, and that there is no creator.

Friedrich Wilhelm Joseph Schelling (1775–1854) was a German idealist philosopher. His works include *System of Transcendental Idealism* (1800) and *The Ages of the World* (1811–15).

F. C. Sibbern (1785–1872) was a professor of philosophy at Copenhagen University.

Socrates (c. 469–399 B.C.E.) was an Athenian philosopher known for his critical conversations with his fellow citizens. Socrates never wrote any of his teachings down, but he has been immortalized in the works of his follower Plato.

WORKS CITED

WORKS CITED

Becker, Ernest. *The Birth and Death of Meaning: An Interdisciplinary Perspective on the Problem of Man*. New York: Free Press, 1971.

———. *The Denial of Death*. New York: Free Press, 1997.

Camus, Albert. *The Rebel: An Essay on Man in Revolt*. New York: Vintage, 1992.

Carlisle, Clare. *Kierkegaard: A Guide for the Perplexed*. London: Bloomsbury, 2006.

———. *Kierkegaard's Philosophy of Becoming: Movements and Positions*. New York: State University of New York Press, 2005.

Cross, Andrew. "Neither Either Nor Or: The Perils of Reflexive Irony." In *The Cambridge Companion to Kierkegaard*, edited by Alastair Hannay and Gordon Daniel Marino, 125–53. Cambridge: Cambridge University Press, 1997.

Crowell, Steven, ed. *The Cambridge Companion to Existentialism*. New York: Cambridge University Press, 2012.

Dreyfus, Hubert L., and Mark A. Wrathall. "A Brief Introduction to Phenomenology and Existentialism." In *A Companion to Phenomenology and Existentialism*, edited by Hubert L. Dreyfus and Mark A. Wrathall. Chichester: John Wiley & Sons, 2011.

———. *A Companion to Phenomenology and Existentialism*. Chichester: John Wiley & Sons, 2011.

Dupré, Louis K. *Kierkegaard as Theologian: The Dialectic of Christian Existence*. New York: Sheed & Ward, 1963.

———. "*The Sickness Unto Death*: Critique of the Modern Age." In *The Existentialists: Critical Essays on Kierkegaard, Nietzsche, Heidegger, and Sartre*, edited by in Charles Guignon. Lanham, MD: Rowman & Littlefield, 2004.

Evans, C. Stephen. *Søren Kierkegaard's Christian Psychology: Insight for Counseling and Pastoral Care*. Grand Rapids, MI: Ministry Resources Library, 1990.

Furtak, Rick Anthony. "Ernest Becker: A Kierkegaardian Theorist of Death and Human Nature." In *Kierkegaard's Influence on the Social Sciences*. Kierkegaard Research: Sources, Reception and Resources, Vol. 13, edited by Jon Bartley Stewart. Farnham: Ashgate Publishing, 2011.

Garff, Joakim. *Søren Kierkegaard: A Biography*. Translated by Bruce H. Kirmmse. Princeton: Princeton University Press, 2007.

Guignon, Charles, ed. *The Existentialists: Critical Essays on Kierkegaard, Nietzsche, Heidegger, and Sartre*. Lanham, MD: Rowman & Littlefield, 2004.

Hannay, Alastair. *Kierkegaard: A Biography*. Cambridge: Cambridge University Press, 2003.

Hannay, Alastair, and Gordon Daniel Marino, eds. *The Cambridge Companion to Kierkegaard*. Cambridge: Cambridge University Press, 1997.

Hegel, Georg Wilhelm Friedrich. *Hegel: Lectures on the Philosophy of Religion: Vol I: Introduction and the Concept of Religion*. Edited by Peter C. Hodgson. Oxford: Oxford University Press, 2007.

———. *Lectures on the Philosophy of World History*. Cambridge: Cambridge University Press, 1975.

———. *Phenomenology of Spirit*. Translated by A. V. Miller. Oxford: Clarendon Press, 1977.

Heidegger, Martin. *Being and Time*. Translated by J. Macquarrie and E. Robinson. Oxford: Basil Blackwell, 1962.

Hong, Howard V., and Edna H. Hong, eds. *The Essential Kierkegaard*. Princeton: Princeton University Press, 2000.

Joseph, Felicity, Jack Reynolds, and Ashley Woodward. *The Bloomsbury Companion to Existentialism*. London: Bloomsbury Publishing, 2014.

Kaufmann, Walter. *Hegel: A Reinterpretation*. Notre Dame, Ind: University of Notre Dame Press, 1988.

Kierkegaard, Søren. *Concluding Unscientific Postscript to Philosophical Fragments, Volume 1*. Translated by Howard V. Hong and Edna H. Hong. Princeton University Press, 1992.

———. *Kierkegaard's Writings, II: The Concept of Irony, with Continual Reference to Socrates/Notes of Schelling's Berlin Lectures*. Edited by Howard V. Hong and Edna H. Hong. Princeton: Princeton University Press, 1992.

———. *Kierkegaard's Writings, VIII: Concept of Anxiety: A Simple Psychologically Orienting Deliberation on the Dogmatic Issue of Hereditary Sin*. Translated by Reidar Thomte. Princeton: Princeton University Press, 1981.

———. *Kierkegaard's Writings, XI: Stages on Life's Way.* Edited by Howard V. Hong and Edna H. Hong. Princeton: Princeton University Press, 2013.

———. *Kierkegaard's Writings, XII: Concluding Unscientific Postscript to Philosophical Fragments*. Edited by Howard V. Hong and Edna H. Hong. Princeton: Princeton University Press, 2013.

———. *Kierkegaard's Writings, XX: Practice in Christianity*. Translated by Howard V. Hong and Edna H. Hong. Princeton: Princeton University Press, 1991.

———. *Kierkegaard's Writings, XXI: For Self-Examination/Judge for Yourself!* Edited by Howard V. Hong and Edna H. Hong. Princeton: Princeton University Press, 1991.

———. *Kierkegaard's Writings: Either/Or Part I*. Edited by Howard V. Hong and Edna H. Hong. Princeton: Princeton University Press, 1988.

———. *The Moment and Late Writings: Kierkegaard's Writings, Vol. 23*. Translated by Howard V. Hong and Edna H. Hong. Princeton: Princeton University Press, 1998.

——— [Anti-Climacus, pseud.]. *The Sickness Unto Death: A Christian Psychological Exposition for Edification and Awakening*. Translated by Alastair Hannay. London: Penguin Classics, 1989.

Kierkegaard, Søren, and H. A. Johnson. *Attack Upon Christendom*. Translated by Walter Macon Lowrie. Princeton: Princeton University Press, 1968.

Kirmmse, Bruce H. *Kierkegaard in Golden Age Denmark*. Bloomington, Ind.: Indiana University Press, 1990.

Lippitt, John. "Eric Fromm: The Integrity of the Self and the Practice of Love." In *Kierkegaard's Influence on the Social Sciences.* Kierkegaard Research: Sources, Reception and Resources, Vol. 13, edited by Jon Bartley Stewart, 95–119. Farnham: Ashgate Publishing, 2011.

Martin, Clancy. "Religious Existentialism." In *A Companion to Phenomenology and Existentialism*, edited by Hubert L. Dreyfus and Mark A. Wrathall, 118–205. Chichester: John Wiley & Sons, 2011.

McDonald, William. "Søren Kierkegaard." In *The Stanford Encyclopedia of Philosophy* (Fall 2012), edited by E. N. Zalta. Accessed 31 July 2015. http://plato.stanford.edu/archives/fall2012/entries/kierkegaard/.

Perkins, Robert L. "Hegel and Kierkegaard: Two Critics of Romantic Irony." *Review of National Literatures* 1, no. 2 (Fall 1970): 250–1.

———. *Søren Kierkegaard*. London: Lutterworth Press, 1969.

Poole, Roger. *Kierkegaard: The Indirect Communication*. Charlottesville: University of Virginia Press, 1993.

Rohde, Peter. *Søren Kierkegaard: An Introduction to His Life and Philosophy*. Translated by Alan Moray Williams. London: Allen & Unwin, 1963.

Sartre, Jean-Paul. *Being and Nothingness*. Translated by Hazel E. Barnes. New York: Washington Square Press, 1993.

Speight, Allen. *The Philosophy of Hegel*. Montreal: McGill Queens University Press, 2008.

Stewart, Jon Bartley, ed. *Kierkegaard and Existentialism*. Farnham: Ashgate Publishing, 2011.

———. *Kierkegaard's Influence on the Social Sciences*. Kierkegaard Research: Sources, Reception and Resources, Vol. 13. Farnham: Ashgate Publishing, 2011.

Taylor, Charles. *A Secular Age*. Cambridge, MA: Harvard University Press, 2007.

Taylor, Mark C. *Journeys to Selfhood: Hegel and Kierkegaard*. New York: Fordham University Press, 2000.

Walsh, Sylvia. *Kierkegaard: Thinking Christianly in an Existential Mode*. Oxford: Oxford University Press, 2009.

Watkin, Julia. *The A to Z of Kierkegaard's Philosophy*. Lanham, MD: Scarecrow Press, 2000.

———. *Kierkegaard*. London: Geoffrey Chapman, 1997.

Weston, Michael. *Kierkegaard and Modern Continental Philosophy: An Introduction*. London: Routledge, 1994.

Westphal, Merold. "Kierkegaard and Hegel." In *The Cambridge Companion to Kierkegaard*, edited by Alastair Hannay and Gordon Daniel Marino, 101–24. Cambridge: Cambridge University Press, 1997.

THE MACAT LIBRARY
BY DISCIPLINE

The Macat Library By Discipline

AFRICANA STUDIES

Chinua Achebe's *An Image of Africa: Racism in Conrad's Heart of Darkness*
W. E. B. Du Bois's *The Souls of Black Folk*
Zora Neale Huston's *Characteristics of Negro Expression*
Martin Luther King Jr's *Why We Can't Wait*
Toni Morrison's *Playing in the Dark: Whiteness in the American Literary Imagination*

ANTHROPOLOGY

Arjun Appadurai's *Modernity at Large: Cultural Dimensions of Globalisation*
Philippe Ariès's *Centuries of Childhood*
Franz Boas's *Race, Language and Culture*
Kim Chan & Renée Mauborgne's *Blue Ocean Strategy*
Jared Diamond's *Guns, Germs & Steel: the Fate of Human Societies*
Jared Diamond's *Collapse: How Societies Choose to Fail or Survive*
E. E. Evans-Pritchard's *Witchcraft, Oracles and Magic Among the Azande*
James Ferguson's *The Anti-Politics Machine*
Clifford Geertz's *The Interpretation of Cultures*
David Graeber's *Debt: the First 5000 Years*
Karen Ho's *Liquidated: An Ethnography of Wall Street*
Geert Hofstede's *Culture's Consequences: Comparing Values, Behaviors, Institutes and Organizations across Nations*
Claude Lévi-Strauss's *Structural Anthropology*
Jay Macleod's *Ain't No Makin' It: Aspirations and Attainment in a Low-Income Neighborhood*
Saba Mahmood's *The Politics of Piety: The Islamic Revival and the Feminist Subject*
Marcel Mauss's *The Gift*

BUSINESS

Jean Lave & Etienne Wenger's *Situated Learning*
Theodore Levitt's *Marketing Myopia*
Burton G. Malkiel's *A Random Walk Down Wall Street*
Douglas McGregor's *The Human Side of Enterprise*
Michael Porter's *Competitive Strategy: Creating and Sustaining Superior Performance*
John Kotter's *Leading Change*
C. K. Prahalad & Gary Hamel's *The Core Competence of the Corporation*

CRIMINOLOGY

Michelle Alexander's *The New Jim Crow: Mass Incarceration in the Age of Colorblindness*
Michael R. Gottfredson & Travis Hirschi's *A General Theory of Crime*
Richard Herrnstein & Charles A. Murray's *The Bell Curve: Intelligence and Class Structure in American Life*
Elizabeth Loftus's *Eyewitness Testimony*
Jay Macleod's *Ain't No Makin' It: Aspirations and Attainment in a Low-Income Neighborhood*
Philip Zimbardo's *The Lucifer Effect*

ECONOMICS

Janet Abu-Lughod's *Before European Hegemony*
Ha-Joon Chang's *Kicking Away the Ladder*
David Brion Davis's *The Problem of Slavery in the Age of Revolution*
Milton Friedman's *The Role of Monetary Policy*
Milton Friedman's *Capitalism and Freedom*
David Graeber's *Debt: the First 5000 Years*
Friedrich Hayek's *The Road to Serfdom*
Karen Ho's *Liquidated: An Ethnography of Wall Street*

The Macat Library By Discipline

John Maynard Keynes's *The General Theory of Employment, Interest and Money*
Charles P. Kindleberger's *Manias, Panics and Crashes*
Robert Lucas's *Why Doesn't Capital Flow from Rich to Poor Countries?*
Burton G. Malkiel's *A Random Walk Down Wall Street*
Thomas Robert Malthus's *An Essay on the Principle of Population*
Karl Marx's *Capital*
Thomas Piketty's *Capital in the Twenty-First Century*
Amartya Sen's *Development as Freedom*
Adam Smith's *The Wealth of Nations*
Nassim Nicholas Taleb's *The Black Swan: The Impact of the Highly Improbable*
Amos Tversky's & Daniel Kahneman's *Judgment under Uncertainty: Heuristics and Biases*
Mahbub Ul Haq's *Reflections on Human Development*
Max Weber's *The Protestant Ethic and the Spirit of Capitalism*

FEMINISM AND GENDER STUDIES

Judith Butler's *Gender Trouble*
Simone De Beauvoir's *The Second Sex*
Michel Foucault's *History of Sexuality*
Betty Friedan's *The Feminine Mystique*
Saba Mahmood's *The Politics of Piety: The Islamic Revival and the Feminist Subjec*t
Joan Wallach Scott's *Gender and the Politics of History*
Mary Wollstonecraft's *A Vindication of the Rights of Woman*
Virginia Woolf's *A Room of One's Own*

GEOGRAPHY

The Brundtland Report's *Our Common Future*
Rachel Carson's *Silent Spring*
Charles Darwin's *On the Origin of Species*
James Ferguson's *The Anti-Politics Machine*
Jane Jacobs's *The Death and Life of Great American Cities*
James Lovelock's *Gaia: A New Look at Life on Earth*
Amartya Sen's *Development as Freedom*
Mathis Wackernagel & William Rees's *Our Ecological Footprint*

HISTORY

Janet Abu-Lughod's *Before European Hegemony*
Benedict Anderson's *Imagined Communities*
Bernard Bailyn's *The Ideological Origins of the American Revolution*
Hanna Batatu's *The Old Social Classes And The Revolutionary Movements Of Iraq*
Christopher Browning's *Ordinary Men: Reserve Police Batallion 101 and the Final Solution in Poland*
Edmund Burke's *Reflections on the Revolution in France*
William Cronon's *Nature's Metropolis: Chicago And The Great West*
Alfred W. Crosby's *The Columbian Exchange*
Hamid Dabashi's *Iran: A People Interrupted*
David Brion Davis's *The Problem of Slavery in the Age of Revolution*
Nathalie Zemon Davis's *The Return of Martin Guerre*
Jared Diamond's *Guns, Germs & Steel: the Fate of Human Societies*
Frank Dikotter's *Mao's Great Famine*
John W Dower's *War Without Mercy: Race And Power In The Pacific War*
W. E. B. Du Bois's *The Souls of Black Folk*
Richard J. Evans's *In Defence of History*
Lucien Febvre's *The Problem of Unbelief in the 16th Century*
Sheila Fitzpatrick's *Everyday Stalinism*

Eric Foner's *Reconstruction: America's Unfinished Revolution, 1863-1877*
Michel Foucault's *Discipline and Punish*
Michel Foucault's *History of Sexuality*
Francis Fukuyama's *The End of History and the Last Man*
John Lewis Gaddis's *We Now Know: Rethinking Cold War History*
Ernest Gellner's *Nations and Nationalism*
Eugene Genovese's *Roll, Jordan, Roll: The World the Slaves Made*
Carlo Ginzburg's *The Night Battles*
Daniel Goldhagen's *Hitler's Willing Executioners*
Jack Goldstone's *Revolution and Rebellion in the Early Modern World*
Antonio Gramsci's *The Prison Notebooks*
Alexander Hamilton, John Jay & James Madison's *The Federalist Papers*
Christopher Hill's *The World Turned Upside Down*
Carole Hillenbrand's *The Crusades: Islamic Perspectives*
Thomas Hobbes's *Leviathan*
Eric Hobsbawm's *The Age Of Revolution*
John A. Hobson's *Imperialism: A Study*
Albert Hourani's *History of the Arab Peoples*
Samuel P. Huntington's *The Clash of Civilizations and the Remaking of World Order*
C. L. R. James's *The Black Jacobins*
Tony Judt's *Postwar: A History of Europe Since 1945*
Ernst Kantorowicz's *The King's Two Bodies: A Study in Medieval Political Theology*
Paul Kennedy's *The Rise and Fall of the Great Powers*
Ian Kershaw's *The "Hitler Myth": Image and Reality in the Third Reich*
John Maynard Keynes's *The General Theory of Employment, Interest and Money*
Charles P. Kindleberger's *Manias, Panics and Crashes*
Martin Luther King Jr's *Why We Can't Wait*
Henry Kissinger's *World Order: Reflections on the Character of Nations and the Course of History*
Thomas Kuhn's *The Structure of Scientific Revolutions*
Georges Lefebvre's *The Coming of the French Revolution*
John Locke's *Two Treatises of Government*
Niccolò Machiavelli's *The Prince*
Thomas Robert Malthus's *An Essay on the Principle of Population*
Mahmood Mamdani's *Citizen and Subject: Contemporary Africa And The Legacy Of Late Colonialism*
Karl Marx's *Capital*
Stanley Milgram's *Obedience to Authority*
John Stuart Mill's *On Liberty*
Thomas Paine's *Common Sense*
Thomas Paine's *Rights of Man*
Geoffrey Parker's *Global Crisis: War, Climate Change and Catastrophe in the Seventeenth Century*
Jonathan Riley-Smith's *The First Crusade and the Idea of Crusading*
Jean-Jacques Rousseau's *The Social Contract*
Joan Wallach Scott's *Gender and the Politics of History*
Theda Skocpol's *States and Social Revolutions*
Adam Smith's *The Wealth of Nations*
Timothy Snyder's *Bloodlands: Europe Between Hitler and Stalin*
Sun Tzu's *The Art of War*
Keith Thomas's *Religion and the Decline of Magic*
Thucydides's *The History of the Peloponnesian War*
Frederick Jackson Turner's *The Significance of the Frontier in American History*
Odd Arne Westad's *The Global Cold War: Third World Interventions And The Making Of Our Times*

The Macat Library By Discipline

LITERATURE

Chinua Achebe's *An Image of Africa: Racism in Conrad's Heart of Darkness*
Roland Barthes's *Mythologies*
Homi K. Bhabha's *The Location of Culture*
Judith Butler's *Gender Trouble*
Simone De Beauvoir's *The Second Sex*
Ferdinand De Saussure's *Course in General Linguistics*
T. S. Eliot's *The Sacred Wood: Essays on Poetry and Criticism*
Zora Neale Huston's *Characteristics of Negro Expression*
Toni Morrison's *Playing in the Dark: Whiteness in the American Literary Imagination*
Edward Said's *Orientalism*
Gayatri Chakravorty Spivak's *Can the Subaltern Speak?*
Mary Wollstonecraft's *A Vindication of the Rights of Women*
Virginia Woolf's *A Room of One's Own*

PHILOSOPHY

Elizabeth Anscombe's *Modern Moral Philosophy*
Hannah Arendt's *The Human Condition*
Aristotle's *Metaphysics*
Aristotle's *Nicomachean Ethics*
Edmund Gettier's *Is Justified True Belief Knowledge?*
Georg Wilhelm Friedrich Hegel's *Phenomenology of Spirit*
David Hume's *Dialogues Concerning Natural Religion*
David Hume's *The Enquiry for Human Understanding*
Immanuel Kant's *Religion within the Boundaries of Mere Reason*
Immanuel Kant's *Critique of Pure Reason*
Søren Kierkegaard's *The Sickness Unto Death*
Søren Kierkegaard's *Fear and Trembling*
C. S. Lewis's *The Abolition of Man*
Alasdair MacIntyre's *After Virtue*
Marcus Aurelius's *Meditations*
Friedrich Nietzsche's *On the Genealogy of Morality*
Friedrich Nietzsche's *Beyond Good and Evil*
Plato's *Republic*
Plato's *Symposium*
Jean-Jacques Rousseau's *The Social Contract*
Gilbert Ryle's *The Concept of Mind*
Baruch Spinoza's *Ethics*
Sun Tzu's *The Art of War*
Ludwig Wittgenstein's *Philosophical Investigations*

POLITICS

Benedict Anderson's *Imagined Communities*
Aristotle's *Politics*
Bernard Bailyn's *The Ideological Origins of the American Revolution*
Edmund Burke's *Reflections on the Revolution in France*
John C. Calhoun's *A Disquisition on Government*
Ha-Joon Chang's *Kicking Away the Ladder*
Hamid Dabashi's *Iran: A People Interrupted*
Hamid Dabashi's *Theology of Discontent: The Ideological Foundation of the Islamic Revolution in Iran*
Robert Dahl's *Democracy and its Critics*
Robert Dahl's *Who Governs?*
David Brion Davis's *The Problem of Slavery in the Age of Revolution*

Alexis De Tocqueville's *Democracy in America*
James Ferguson's *The Anti-Politics Machine*
Frank Dikotter's *Mao's Great Famine*
Sheila Fitzpatrick's *Everyday Stalinism*
Eric Foner's *Reconstruction: America's Unfinished Revolution, 1863-1877*
Milton Friedman's *Capitalism and Freedom*
Francis Fukuyama's *The End of History and the Last Man*
John Lewis Gaddis's *We Now Know: Rethinking Cold War History*
Ernest Gellner's *Nations and Nationalism*
David Graeber's *Debt: the First 5000 Years*
Antonio Gramsci's *The Prison Notebooks*
Alexander Hamilton, John Jay & James Madison's *The Federalist Papers*
Friedrich Hayek's *The Road to Serfdom*
Christopher Hill's *The World Turned Upside Down*
Thomas Hobbes's *Leviathan*
John A. Hobson's *Imperialism: A Study*
Samuel P. Huntington's *The Clash of Civilizations and the Remaking of World Order*
Tony Judt's *Postwar: A History of Europe Since 1945*
David C. Kang's *China Rising: Peace, Power and Order in East Asia*
Paul Kennedy's *The Rise and Fall of Great Powers*
Robert Keohane's *After Hegemony*
Martin Luther King Jr.'s *Why We Can't Wait*
Henry Kissinger's *World Order: Reflections on the Character of Nations and the Course of History*
John Locke's *Two Treatises of Government*
Niccolò Machiavelli's *The Prince*
Thomas Robert Malthus's *An Essay on the Principle of Population*
Mahmood Mamdani's *Citizen and Subject: Contemporary Africa And The Legacy Of Late Colonialism*
Karl Marx's *Capital*
John Stuart Mill's *On Liberty*
John Stuart Mill's *Utilitarianism*
Hans Morgenthau's *Politics Among Nations*
Thomas Paine's *Common Sense*
Thomas Paine's *Rights of Man*
Thomas Piketty's *Capital in the Twenty-First Century*
Robert D. Putman's *Bowling Alone*
John Rawls's *Theory of Justice*
Jean-Jacques Rousseau's *The Social Contract*
Theda Skocpol's *States and Social Revolutions*
Adam Smith's *The Wealth of Nations*
Sun Tzu's *The Art of War*
Henry David Thoreau's *Civil Disobedience*
Thucydides's *The History of the Peloponnesian War*
Kenneth Waltz's *Theory of International Politics*
Max Weber's *Politics as a Vocation*
Odd Arne Westad's *The Global Cold War: Third World Interventions And The Making Of Our Times*

POSTCOLONIAL STUDIES

Roland Barthes's *Mythologies*
Frantz Fanon's *Black Skin, White Masks*
Homi K. Bhabha's *The Location of Culture*
Gustavo Gutiérrez's *A Theology of Liberation*
Edward Said's *Orientalism*
Gayatri Chakravorty Spivak's *Can the Subaltern Speak?*

The Macat Library By Discipline

PSYCHOLOGY

Gordon Allport's *The Nature of Prejudice*
Alan Baddeley & Graham Hitch's *Aggression: A Social Learning Analysis*
Albert Bandura's *Aggression: A Social Learning Analysis*
Leon Festinger's *A Theory of Cognitive Dissonance*
Sigmund Freud's *The Interpretation of Dreams*
Betty Friedan's *The Feminine Mystique*
Michael R. Gottfredson & Travis Hirschi's *A General Theory of Crime*
Eric Hoffer's *The True Believer: Thoughts on the Nature of Mass Movements*
William James's *Principles of Psychology*
Elizabeth Loftus's *Eyewitness Testimony*
A. H. Maslow's *A Theory of Human Motivation*
Stanley Milgram's *Obedience to Authority*
Steven Pinker's *The Better Angels of Our Nature*
Oliver Sacks's *The Man Who Mistook His Wife For a Hat*
Richard Thaler & Cass Sunstein's *Nudge: Improving Decisions About Health, Wealth and Happiness*
Amos Tversky's *Judgment under Uncertainty: Heuristics and Biases*
Philip Zimbardo's *The Lucifer Effect*

SCIENCE

Rachel Carson's *Silent Spring*
William Cronon's *Nature's Metropolis: Chicago And The Great West*
Alfred W. Crosby's *The Columbian Exchange*
Charles Darwin's *On the Origin of Species*
Richard Dawkin's *The Selfish Gene*
Thomas Kuhn's *The Structure of Scientific Revolutions*
Geoffrey Parker's *Global Crisis: War, Climate Change and Catastrophe in the Seventeenth Century*
Mathis Wackernagel & William Rees's *Our Ecological Footprint*

SOCIOLOGY

Michelle Alexander's *The New Jim Crow: Mass Incarceration in the Age of Colorblindness*
Gordon Allport's *The Nature of Prejudice*
Albert Bandura's *Aggression: A Social Learning Analysis*
Hanna Batatu's *The Old Social Classes And The Revolutionary Movements Of Iraq*
Ha-Joon Chang's *Kicking Away the Ladder*
W. E. B. Du Bois's *The Souls of Black Folk*
Émile Durkheim's *On Suicide*
Frantz Fanon's *Black Skin, White Masks*
Frantz Fanon's *The Wretched of the Earth*
Eric Foner's *Reconstruction: America's Unfinished Revolution, 1863-1877*
Eugene Genovese's *Roll, Jordan, Roll: The World the Slaves Made*
Jack Goldstone's *Revolution and Rebellion in the Early Modern World*
Antonio Gramsci's *The Prison Notebooks*
Richard Herrnstein & Charles A Murray's *The Bell Curve: Intelligence and Class Structure in American Life*
Eric Hoffer's *The True Believer: Thoughts on the Nature of Mass Movements*
Jane Jacobs's *The Death and Life of Great American Cities*
Robert Lucas's *Why Doesn't Capital Flow from Rich to Poor Countries?*
Jay Macleod's *Ain't No Makin' It: Aspirations and Attainment in a Low Income Neighborhood*
Elaine May's *Homeward Bound: American Families in the Cold War Era*
Douglas McGregor's *The Human Side of Enterprise*
C. Wright Mills's *The Sociological Imagination*

Thomas Piketty's *Capital in the Twenty-First Century*
Robert D. Putman's *Bowling Alone*
David Riesman's *The Lonely Crowd: A Study of the Changing American Character*
Edward Said's *Orientalism*
Joan Wallach Scott's *Gender and the Politics of History*
Theda Skocpol's *States and Social Revolutions*
Max Weber's *The Protestant Ethic and the Spirit of Capitalism*

THEOLOGY

Augustine's *Confessions*
Benedict's *Rule of St Benedict*
Gustavo Gutiérrez's *A Theology of Liberation*
Carole Hillenbrand's *The Crusades: Islamic Perspectives*
David Hume's *Dialogues Concerning Natural Religion*
Immanuel Kant's *Religion within the Boundaries of Mere Reason*
Ernst Kantorowicz's *The King's Two Bodies: A Study in Medieval Political Theology*
Søren Kierkegaard's *The Sickness Unto Death*
C. S. Lewis's *The Abolition of Man*
Saba Mahmood's *The Politics of Piety: The Islamic Revival and the Feminist Subject*
Baruch Spinoza's *Ethics*
Keith Thomas's *Religion and the Decline of Magic*

COMING SOON

Chris Argyris's *The Individual and the Organisation*
Seyla Benhabib's *The Rights of Others*
Walter Benjamin's *The Work Of Art in the Age of Mechanical Reproduction*
John Berger's *Ways of Seeing*
Pierre Bourdieu's *Outline of a Theory of Practice*
Mary Douglas's *Purity and Danger*
Roland Dworkin's *Taking Rights Seriously*
James G. March's *Exploration and Exploitation in Organisational Learning*
Ikujiro Nonaka's *A Dynamic Theory of Organizational Knowledge Creation*
Griselda Pollock's *Vision and Difference*
Amartya Sen's *Inequality Re-Examined*
Susan Sontag's *On Photography*
Yasser Tabbaa's *The Transformation of Islamic Art*
Ludwig von Mises's *Theory of Money and Credit*

The Macat Library By Discipline

Macat Disciplines

Access the greatest ideas and thinkers across entire disciplines, including

Postcolonial Studies

Roland Barthes's *Mythologies*
Frantz Fanon's *Black Skin, White Masks*
Homi K. Bhabha's *The Location of Culture*
Gustavo Gutiérrez's *A Theology of Liberation*
Edward Said's *Orientalism*
Gayatri Chakravorty Spivak's *Can the Subaltern Speak?*

Macat analyses are available from all good bookshops and libraries.

Access hundreds of analyses through one, multimedia tool.
Join free for one month **library.macat.com**

Macat Disciplines

Access the greatest ideas and thinkers across entire disciplines, including

AFRICANA STUDIES

Chinua Achebe's *An Image of Africa: Racism in Conrad's Heart of Darkness*

W. E. B. Du Bois's *The Souls of Black Folk*

Zora Neale Hurston's *Characteristics of Negro Expression*

Martin Luther King Jr.'s *Why We Can't Wait*

Toni Morrison's *Playing in the Dark: Whiteness in the American Literary Imagination*

Macat analyses are available from all good bookshops and libraries.

Access hundreds of analyses through one, multimedia tool.

Join free for one month **library.macat.com**

Macat Disciplines

Access the greatest ideas and thinkers across entire disciplines, including

FEMINISM, GENDER AND QUEER STUDIES

Simone De Beauvoir's
The Second Sex

Michel Foucault's
History of Sexuality

Betty Friedan's
The Feminine Mystique

Saba Mahmood's
*The Politics of Piety:
The Islamic Revival and
the Feminist Subject*

Joan Wallach Scott's
*Gender and the
Politics of History*

Mary Wollstonecraft's
*A Vindication of the
Rights of Woman*

Virginia Woolf's
A Room of One's Own

Judith Butler's
Gender Trouble

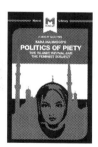

Macat analyses are available from all good bookshops and libraries.

Access hundreds of analyses through one, multimedia tool.
Join free for one month **library.macat.com**

Macat Disciplines

Access the greatest ideas and thinkers across entire disciplines, including

CRIMINOLOGY

Michelle Alexander's
*The New Jim Crow:
Mass Incarceration in the
Age of Colorblindness*

**Michael R. Gottfredson
& Travis Hirschi's**
A General Theory of Crime

Elizabeth Loftus's
Eyewitness Testimony

**Richard Herrnstein
& Charles A. Murray's**
*The Bell Curve: Intelligence and
Class Structure in American Life*

Jay Macleod's
*Ain't No Makin' It:
Aspirations and Attainment in a
Low-Income Neighborhood*

Philip Zimbardo's
The Lucifer Effect

Macat Disciplines

Access the greatest ideas and thinkers across entire disciplines, including

INEQUALITY

Ha-Joon Chang's, *Kicking Away the Ladder*

David Graeber's, *Debt: The First 5000 Years*

Robert E. Lucas's, *Why Doesn't Capital Flow from Rich To Poor Countries?*

Thomas Piketty's, *Capital in the Twenty-First Century*

Amartya Sen's, *Inequality Re-Examined*

Mahbub Ul Haq's, *Reflections on Human Development*

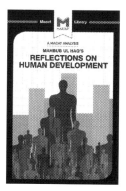

Macat analyses are available from all good bookshops and libraries.

Access hundreds of analyses through one, multimedia tool.
Join free for one month **library.macat.com**

Macat Disciplines

Access the greatest ideas and thinkers across entire disciplines, including

GLOBALIZATION

Arjun Appadurai's, *Modernity at Large: Cultural Dimensions of Globalisation*

James Ferguson's, *The Anti-Politics Machine*

Geert Hofstede's, *Culture's Consequences*

Amartya Sen's, *Development as Freedom*

Macat Disciplines

Access the greatest ideas and thinkers across entire disciplines, including

MAN AND THE ENVIRONMENT

The Brundtland Report's, *Our Common Future*
Rachel Carson's, *Silent Spring*
James Lovelock's, *Gaia: A New Look at Life on Earth*
Mathis Wackernagel & William Rees's, *Our Ecological Footprint*

Macat analyses are available from all good bookshops and libraries.

Access hundreds of analyses through one, multimedia tool.
Join free for one month **library.macat.com**

Printed in the United States
by Baker & Taylor Publisher Services